The Happy Ship

In the same series

THE WHEELING STARS

THE HAPPY SHIP

*Victuals and Vitals
for Yacht Crews*

Kitty Hampton

faber and faber
LONDON · BOSTON

To Desmond, with love

First published in 1989

by Faber and Faber Limited
3 Queen Square London WC1N 3AU

Phototypeset by Input Typesetting Ltd, London
Printed in Great Britain by Richard Clay Ltd, Bungay, Suffolk

A CIP record for this book is available from the British Library

ISBN 0-571-15376-3

Contents

Contents

List of illustrations

Foreword

Last year, somewhere off north-west Scotland, our Nautical Almanac made a wild leap out of its bookshelf and landed in the sink, squashing a pound of tomatoes as it fell. Meanwhile, somewhere beneath the quarterbunk, a packet of dumpling-mix which had been pecked open by a seagull on Portpatrick quay began stealthily to mix itself with a leaking carton of orange juice, producing a new and startling variety of roseate dumpling *à la* cardboard. These incidents, curiously, seemed to make the wind stronger and colder, and the waves more threatening. There is a lot more to successful sailing than ever goes on above decks.

The trouble is, there are far too many books written about how to make boats go faster and not nearly enough on how to make them comfortable. Yet nothing is more vital to a boat than its crew: without alert and competent people aboard the most advanced wing-keel, crafty spinnaker or tactical nav-computer is junk. And it is equally true that human beings, however fit and determined, do not function at their best when fed on disgusting food and clothed in clammy underwear which fell out of its locker into the bilge. Nor is the skipper's clarity of thought likely to be enhanced if the night has been blighted by the clanking of ill-stowed tins and the smell of a mildewed pillow.

So this book, with Kitty Hampton's close attention to the domestic side of yachting – stowage, victualling, health and entertainment – is more than welcome. Particularly so because she is no mere 'cruising wife', likely to make such shocking suggestions as heaving-to for lunch in the middle of a race, borrowing the navigator's dividers to pick crabmeat, or staying in harbour in anything above Force 4. As a seasoned racing crew and skipper in her own right, Kitty accepts with equanimity the prospect of living at a silly angle for days on end, and will probably be found tranquilly marinading mackerel in gin under conditions in which most of us would serve up only a sandwich and a snarl. Her knowledge of everything from sailcloth to *court bouillon* makes her an authority to be bowed to by even the most fanatical racing skipper, and an invaluable guide and inspiration to us weaker brethren.

Libby Purves

Introduction and Acknowledgements

This book is for anyone who has ever stood beside their boat on a Friday evening with several trolleys crammed with cases of food, boxes of tools, the kitchen sink, as well as bags of clothes for every eventuality: in short, the incredible amount of gear that looks as if you are leaving home for good, when all you are doing is going sailing for a long weekend. Inevitably it will be raining, and somehow all that kit has to be fitted into the boat before it gets soaked. Just as you have heaved the last case aboard, someone appears with another armful of carrier bags and three more pairs of boots. The skipper, who has just got off the train from work, is in a hurry to get to sea so that he doesn't miss the tide. As you cast off and begin motoring down the river, someone shouts to inform you: 'Supper under way in about thirty minutes will be just fine.' Meanwhile, bulky bags and boxes have still to be jammed into already bulging lockers before you can pour yourself that much needed gin. Suddenly the engine coughs and wheezes into silence. Someone shouts, 'Pass the mole wrench and the torch – quickly.' Within seconds the saloon looks like the inside of a tumble-drier as everything whirls around.

I hope that this book may provide a little help with the planning of what to take and where on earth to put it, making the best use of available space, and how to find it again. The key to running a happy ship is a certain amount of pre-planning before the start of the season or before a long passage, so that should things go wrong (and even on the best planned boats they do), the solution has been thought out beforehand – the 'what if' factor. It is not like planning a military exercise; too much rigidity is certain to dampen the spirits of the crew, and good morale is vital. A happy crew is the sign of a well-run ship.

Much can be done to keep morale high by seeing that the crew are fed and watered regularly and that meals are a constant source of interest. With this in mind I have dwelt at some length on how to provide for the crew in different climates and faraway places, with some emphasis on the type of victuals and seafood which may be expected there.

Thanks are due to Nautical Publishing Co. Ltd., an imprint of A. & C. Black (Publishers) Ltd., for permission to reprint the extract from *Ocean Sailing* by Rob James, and to Macmillan Publishers Ltd. for the extract from *North Atlantic Seafood* by Alan Davidson.

My special thanks are to my husband, Desmond, who is a fund of practical advice as well as a constant source of encouragement. I am indebted to a great many sailing friends from whom I have learned a great deal and in particular to those who have contributed to this book with their advice and ideas. In particular: Mary Barton, Andrew Bray, Robin Bryer, Mary Falk, Pat Hesketh, Rachael Hayward, Naomi James, Robin and Sue Knox-Johnston, Betty Linsay-Thomson, Robert Nickerson, Geoff Pack, Hazel and Bill Perks, Simon Rippon, Fred Staibe and Karen White. I should also like to express my very grateful thanks to Libby Purves for writing the foreword, Mike Collins for his excellent illustrations, Dr Maurice Rosen for advising me on matters medical, Mike Peyton for his cartoon on the jacket and, last and by no means least, I should like to thank Captain John Coote, who persuaded me to write this book in the first place and as editor has provided me with so much help and inspiration throughout.

Kitty Hampton
January 1989

CHAPTER ONE

Stowage

'If consequence do but approve my dream
My boat sails freely, both with wind and stream.'
Othello. II.iii.

In Utopia, where money grows on trees and a zephyr breeze is constant in strength as well as direction, we should all no doubt build the boat of our dreams. She would be roomy enough down below to accommodate the family in the fashion that they aspire to. Unfortunately, few of us have access to limitless funds, so we tend to end up with a boat that is a compromise in some way, often modified for someone else with different requirements.

However, there is a great deal to be said for buying a second-hand boat. To begin with, it has probably had most of its bugs discovered and problems solved for you, and previous owners may have made some modifications. Few yachts are built with enough stowage space for its supposedly full complement of crew; the yacht that some smart-looking salesman at a boat show proudly demonstrates as 'sleeps six in the greatest of comfort', rarely, if ever, can show you how and where the six crew are supposed to stow their gear. A few interconnected lockers with sliding doors at the back of the saloon seats is all you will find if you are lucky. There may be space under the seats, but who wants to dig around in these in a heavy sea-way, especially if the cushions are not an integral part of the locker lid. Lockers behind the saloon seats are inaccessible and inconvenient – either too small or too big – and neatly folded clothes become a jumbled heap within a short space of time.

It does not matter whether you are planning a short sail for a few hours or a couple of days, a two-week cruise or even an extended voyage that may last several months, the crew need food and water.

I

It was Samuel Pepys, himself responsible for victualling the Navy for many years, who said:

Englishmen, and more especially seamen, love their bellies above everything else, and therefore it must always be remembered in the management of the victualling of the Navy, that to make any abatement of them in the quantity or agreeableness of their victuals, is to discourage and provoke them in their tenderest point, and will sooner render them disgusted with the king's service than any other hardship that could be put upon them.

Here are two different types of yacht showing interior details such as the lockers and galley, water tanks, suggested stowage plans.

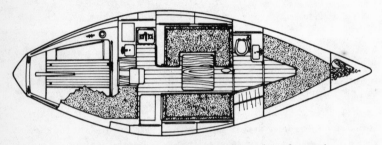

1. The family cruiser – layout for a typical 32-foot yacht

In the last fifteen years or so, yacht design of production cruising boats has been strongly influenced by the IOR rules resulting in far more beamy boats than the Nicholsons, Rivals and the Contessa shape of hull, which by today's standards seem narrow. But it was the French who were the first to realize the potential in designing their cruising yachts around the consumer; clearly what he wanted was something as close as possible to his own home. When the 'First 30' was exhibited at the London Boat Show, no one could get over the fact that it was possible to fit a capacious after cabin in a boat of that length. Perhaps the English are unique in that they seldom appear to go cruising with as many crew as the French seem to cram into what looks an incredibly small space. You only have to sit in a French port and watch the arrival of a small local boat and subsequent disgorgement of her crew: there is one person at the helm, one in the cockpit and two on deck. As they approach their berth two more people appear up the companion steps while another couple pop up through the forward hatch – and those are just the adult members of the crew in a 24 footer.

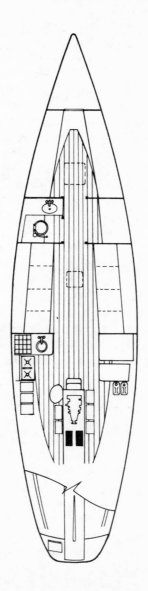

2. A stripped-out, ultra light displacement (ULD) ocean racer

LOCKERS

The chief problem that remains is, how on earth are you going to fit all the gear and clothes, as well as provisions for a couple of months, into the space available? Once stowed, will they be easy to retrieve and will they stay in position in a rough sea? There are several places where space is usually wasted, for example, under the sink. Lockers with sliding doors fore and aft are bad enough, but when you see them athwartships then you know for certain that the designer has not been to sea in one of his own boats. There are one or two simple things that can be done to remedy these snags if previous owners have not done it already for you. It may sound obvious, but has the owner warned the new crew about the lack of space on board? If not, he may end up with the Davis/Carruthers situation so well described in *The Riddle of the Sands*. Cabin trunks are only welcome on board the kind of yachts owned by Greek shipping magnates: there simply is not room on anything less than 75 tonnes. The same applies to golf clubs, umbrellas, prams, pushchairs or even scooters. Some yachts do have capacious enough lockers for folding bicycles but, unless invited to bring it, leave yours behind. The same can be said for windsurfers, waterskis and scuba gear. Unless told otherwise, confine your luggage to foul weather gear, a sleeping bag, one duffel bag and suitable gear for going ashore to respectable restaurants.

The locker under the sink is an area where space can easily be wasted. By attaching to the door a plastic-coated wire basket you gain an extra shelf, likewise a gash bucket if not already installed. These fittings can be easily found in any DIY shop. A cupboard on the fore and aft position can be improved by a series of basket shelves on runners that you pull out on a track. Another alternative is to fit plastic bins on shelves, again bought from a DIY shop (see Fig. 5). These have the advantage over the wire baskets in that they are solid and are strong enough to be used as drawers. Saloon seats where the cushions are not attached to the locker tops: either have new covers made for you that do attach, or sew tape around the cushion cover and staple on to the lid.

The catches on lockers are an important item. Are they magnetic or made of plastic? The magnetic variety are not usually strong enough to withstand the weight of heavy items forcing them open. Plastic catches may work well enough for a season or two, but may not last

3. Gaining extra locker space

as long as the old bronze cockerel type that you work with your finger. There is only one snag with this type of catch; when well heeled, stuff inside the locker may be jammed tight against the catch making it difficult to open. In some cases they can be forced open by the sheer weight of items inside the locker pressing against the catch. The way round this is to fit brass or wooden drawer guards upside-down inside the locker thus protecting the catch (see Fig. 6).

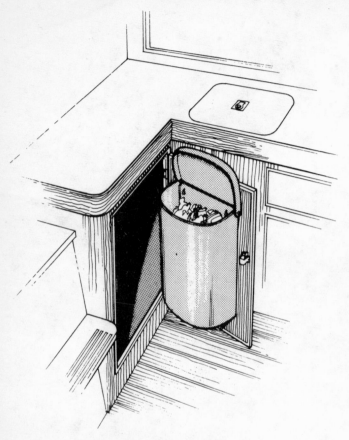

4.   Gash bin attached to locker door

The cushion seats along the sides of benches usually conceal lockers behind them and the cushions are supposed to stay in position with Velcro. In practice they tend to fall off when the boat is well heeled. Since the Velcro wears out easily the solution is to renew it regularly.

Extra stowage space can be made by the use of nets under the bulkhead. They are useful for clothes as well as fruit and vegetables. A simple method is to fix a net on either side of the saloon behind the seats. This should be firmly attached at the bottom with a strong length of elastic at the top.

The beauty of this is that it is easy to see where your socks are,

6

5. Basket shelves on runners

and underneath the deck is usually a dry place. Fruit and vegetables also benefit from this as air circulating round them helps to keep them fresh. Net-type stowage is also invaluable for children's toys and games.

STOWAGE PLANS

It is common sense to stow heavy items as low in your boat as possible. During the 1979 Fastnet Race when the fleet were hit by a sudden exceptionally severe gale, many of the head injuries that occurred resulted from careless stowage of tins and other miscellaneous objects

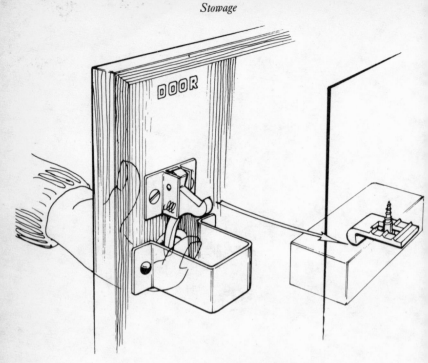

6. Cockerel catch with guard

flying out of lockers. Apart from being as low down as possible, it also makes good sense to have your heaviest items as close as possible to the mast. The obvious place is under the saloon seats. There is space under saloon seats for the bulk of your tins. This also goes for tools and spares as well. Light things such as extra lavatory and kitchen paper sealed in tough polythene bags can be stowed well forward or aft, whichever place is the drier. The best advice is to make a chart showing where each item is kept, and to label the lockers as well. This avoids confusion when a new crew member is asked to find the spare torch in the middle of the night. It is also a good idea to make a stores list and, if you can remember, to cross off each tin as it is consumed. This saves running out of essential items, or wasting time grovelling upside down in the bilges for half an hour in search of that one tin of *foie gras* you thought you had left. A list is invaluable as an *aide mémoire* for planning next year's cruise; if it has been kept up to date, you see at a glance which items were left uneaten.

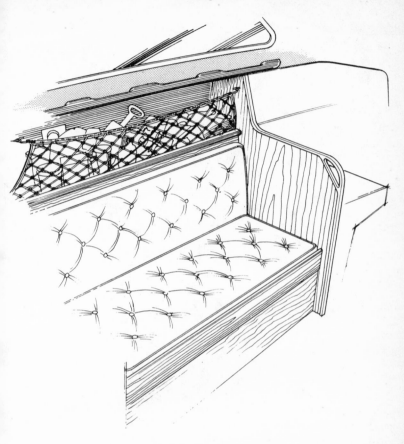

7. Netting behind saloon seats

When sailing with a new crew we make a list and keep it stuck up in the galley showing who drinks tea or coffee, with or without sugar, as well as which kind of hot drinks the crew prefer in the middle of the night. Before the advent of Cup-a-Soups with little bits in them, we used to make our own version from a spoonful of the left-over stew and boiling water, a welcome treat in the middle of a cold night watch, until the skipper found what he thought to be a nice lump of meat in the bottom of his mug: it turned out to be a tea-bag.

Remember, too, that silence is golden when cruising. There is nothing so infuriating as the rattle and irregular chink of loosely

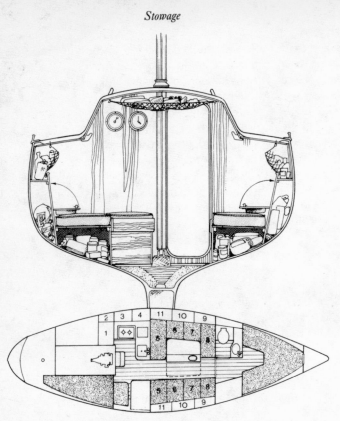

8. Stowage plans with locker lay-out chart

stowed items underneath seats and behind lockers – valuable minutes of sleep can be wasted by having to seek out the recalcitrant article. (The same applies to the tip-tapping of unfrapped halyards.) Pieces of rag or foam padding cut into suitable wedge shapes or used as layers between will stop the irritating noise. The sliding locker doors around the galley are also prone to rattle in an annoying manner; wedges of kitchen paper can be used to prevent this.

Underneath the saloon seats on either side, the space is usually divided into three. One method of planning the stowage is to think of each compartment as holding a week's or a month's supplies at a time (depending obviously on the length of cruise). This is simpler than putting all meat in one, vegetables in another. A point to watch is where you put cardboard cartons of milk or fruit juice. If for any reason you get water into the locker, those cartons are going to get soggy. If heavy tins are likely to bounce about on top of them, it doesn't need much imagination to visualize the ensuing mess. Keep those cartons separated from tins or other heavy objects. A case of longlife milk is somewhat protected from damp by the case itself – if covered in plastic that too will be additional protection. I once made the mistake of stowing four dozen eggs and a dozen cartons of milk in the bows underneath the fo'c'sle berths. This was fine until the boat was knocked down during a severe gale; every egg was smashed, as were some of the cartons of milk. The mess was appalling and the smell of sour milk lingered for weeks.

Stowing gear on deck

Depending on the size of boat and the areas in which you intend to cruise, you may want to take an outboard engine. Stowing the beast can be a nightmare, especially if it is put in the bottom of a huge cockpit locker. Small outboards can easily be stowed by fixing a bracket on the pushpit where they will be quite safe and out of the way. Don't forget to have a secure line to tie it on as well.

Windsurfers or sail boards sit quite happily along the side deck where they are securely fastened to the stanchions. If you think that you are in for a blow, they should be removed and put down below because green water breaking across the deck will carry them away, probably along with the stanchions. Their masts will be quite safe if firmly lashed against the shrouds.

Dinghies and life rafts

If your life raft is in a hard case, then it will not come to any harm on deck. The valise type must be stowed where it will not be damaged by being trampled on or from the effects of wind and weather. If it is stowed in its own made-to-measure locker it is easy for anyone to get it in case of emergency.

Tinker Tramps and Travellers have become increasingly popular with cruising people the world over as they are multi-purpose dinghies. The basic boat makes an excellent ship's tender as not only is it easier to row than other rubber dinghies, but it also performs well under power. With the addition of a mast, sails, dagger board and rudder you have a sailing dinghy which is fun for all the crew. The mast can be stowed inside the dinghy as it is in three sections. With the addition

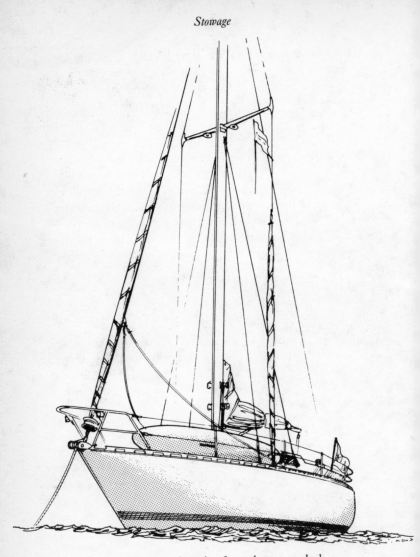

9.   Stowage of windsurfer and mast on deck

of CO_2 bottles, canopy and drogue, you have a fully-equipped survival craft that, should you have to abandon your boat, can be sailed towards safety. Their only disadvantage is that they are heavier and more bulky to stow than other rubber dinghies. If your boat has davits, there is no problem with stowage.

WEIGHT SAVING

(If you are not concerned about carrying extra weight, then you can skip this section).

Owners of cruiser/racers like to compete in the occasional race. For day racing, if they are a competitive lot, they will have already removed anything they do not need. For longer races there are one or two things you can do to avoid carrying unnecessary weight. It is important to keep the ends of the boat as light as possible. The disadvantage of those cavernous cockpit lockers is that they are so big it is easy to cram them with all manner of junk. Take everything out and evaluate what is and what is not going to be needed; you will be surprised at the amount you can leave behind. The cabin table gets in the way, especially when lugging sails through the saloon; it weighs a ton and is far better off in the garage at home. The same is true of the door into the heads. If you take your racing very seriously indeed, decant all jars of jam, pickle and mayonnaise into plastic containers and leave behind all but the bare essentials of cutlery, plates and mugs. Insist that the crew have disposable socks and holes in the handles of their toothbrushes.

CHAPTER TWO

The Galley

'If you can't stand the heat, get out of the kitchen.'
Harry S. Truman

COOKING FUELS AND COOKERS

The most popular form of cooking fuel is gas. The majority of the cookers supplied with boats are made for caravans and marinized simply by fitting gimbals. With two burners, a grill and an oven, they are perfectly adequate. The grill may rust and corrode if it gets regularly doused in salt water, but can be easily replaced. Gas bottles are normally carried in their separate self-draining locker on deck.It is essential that the gas bottle can be turned off at source as well as beside the cooker itself. Everyone is aware of the dangers of leaking gas and there are several gas detectors on the market that are supposed to be able to sniff out a leak. Sometimes they are too sensitive and go off all the time, or, like bloodhounds with sinus trouble, they fail to detect gas when the cooker is turned on but unlit.

The best and the most simple gadget is called Gas-Low. This measures the pressure in the system and tells you if there is a leak. It is fitted to the gas bottle and when the cooker is off opening the bottle will pressurize the system. If the bottle is then turned off, a leak in the system will register by showing a drop in pressure. The flexible hose is the most vulnerable part of the system; it must be of the correct, reinforced type and the connections should be checked annually and replaced if and when necessary.

As everyone knows, gas is heavier than air and therefore sinks into the bilges. One year we did have a gas leakage when we were at Le Palais on Belle Île off South Brittany. With a small bucket we bailed out the gas, which was then carefully poured over the side. The sight of these mad English who appeared to be having a game with an empty bucket was too much for the French and fairly soon we were surrounded by curious onlookers. After a bucket or three the boss decided that the way to test the success or not of our operation was to fill a bottle with water, pour it slowly into the bilge, thus exchanging the water with any remaining gas, and then, with the bottle held at arm's length over the side, light a match. The match spluttered and flared briefly. The French rowed back to their own boats shaking their heads.

Some foreign boats have alcohol-burning stoves, the advantage being that they are light and economical to run. One disadvantage is that the flame is not very hot and therefore takes longer to heat up a kettle. The other is trying to replace the alcohol. Imagine the dismay of the cold and hungry crew who went ashore in Holland to replenish their alcohol. They went into the nearest grocery shop and asked if they sold alcohol. They were redirected to a chemist, where he said he did but, when they produced a two gallon container and asked him to fill it, the good man looked horrified and said, 'We are not allowed to sell alcohol in that quantity, but I have many miniatures which I can sell you.' Laden with five dozen bottles they returned to the boat. They filled the tank of the cooker with some of the alcohol and struck a match. Nothing happened. They tried to clean the jets, but that had no effect; the pressure was right but still they could not get the beastly thing to light. Finally, in desperation they drank the rest of the alcohol.

Paraffin-burning stoves (Primus) are disliked by many as being messy, smelly, temperamental and old-fashioned. Treated properly they are reliable and the new models are more sophisticated and better designed than in the past. There is something very cosy about the gentle hiss of a paraffin stove; it has an advantage that, should the flame be extinguished by a sudden gust of wind, there is no danger of explosion as in the case of a gas stove. Paraffin is increasingly difficult to get in some parts of the world, so many cruising yachtsmen have replaced their cookers with gas. In remoter areas, gas bottles with standard Calor-gas fittings are hard to come by, so it is advisable to take with you a Camping Gaz converter.

Safety in the Galley

This is vital. A crash bar in front of the cooker to stop the cook falling on to it, as well as a strap to lean against, should be fitted as standard on all yachts. There should be fiddles fitted to the top of the stove so that in theory the pots and pans stay there even when the motion is bumpy; in practice they do not, unless they are the type that fit high enough up the sides of the saucepans. Fiddles should have adjustable screws so that they can be moved to fit different-sized pots. Expandable wire shock-cords can also be used to hold the pot by securing it over and thence each end to the stove fiddles. The oven should be secured with a bolt when not in use, and with a pin to secure the door to stop it opening in a sea-way.

A point that is often overlooked is the need to wear suitable clothing while cooking in hot weather. Trade-wind sailing is often boisterous. Accidents have happened because the cook was wearing only a pair of shorts when a pan of boiling water was flung off the top of a wildly swinging stove over unprotected legs. It is safer to wear oilskin trousers

10. Cooker fiddles and wire shock-cord

than risk being scalded. It might be a good idea to have a long PVC apron on board.

STOWING FOOD

Items that are in constant use, such as coffee, tea-bags, Oxo cubes, sugar, sweets and matches, should be easy to get at without having to stir up the contents of the ready-to-use locker every time someone wants to make a cup of tea. One way of doing this is to have old jam jars, or something similar, that slide into clip-on stowage over the galley. Likewise the box of munchies that the crew raid at odd times

11. Clip-on jars

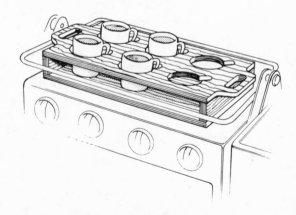

12. Drinks tray

during the day, or night, should also be kept within easy reach of the cockpit. A tray that fits over the top of the cooker with cut-outs for holding cups or glasses is useful when making tea or mixing drinks for a crew of four or more. This saves spilling the tea or Pimms more than necessary, especially when you are on a roller-coaster ride.

For stowing plates and cups, I favour T-shaped racks as they are secure, less likely to rattle and take up less space than if cups and plates are loosely jammed in a locker. All dried food, including packets of cereal are better turned into plastic tubs and sealed in heavy-duty plastic. Small amounts can then be decanted into containers in the ready-to-use locker once or twice a week.

GALLEY EQUIPMENT

The kitchen at home usually bristles with an eclectic array of cooking equipment which we say we cannot possibly live without. The confines of a galley dictate that there is no room for superfluous equipment. Successful cooking at sea requires a certain amount of dexterity and the fewer items you have to juggle with the easier it is. You also learn the hard way that very cheap utensils do not really save you anything in the long run. Apart from getting tatty, they will last no time at all in the destructive environment of the sea; saucepans corrode, the handles come off, and the one and only tin-opener rusts solid. I'm not advocating that you need to rush off and spend a fortune, but consider carefully when you are choosing pots and pans for the boat whether they will stand up to the battering they will get in a galley.

For example, enamel saucepans may look smart on the shelf, but they are bound to get chipped sooner or later. Aluminium corrodes in salt water and very thin saucepans burn easily. Basically you tend to get what you pay for. A kettle with a metal handle and a 'whistle' cover over the spout which has to be removed before you can pour, is my pet *bête noir*. The best kind have a trigger mechanism on the handle that operates the 'whistle' so you can pick up the kettle and pour with one hand. Over the years I have evolved a list of equipment that is basic but efficient whether you are cooking on a one-burner camping gas cooker or one with four burners, a grill and an oven. This list of equipment is in no way mandatory, but fairly comprehensive:

Aluminium foil
Baking tray
Bottle opener – Fixed on bulkhead
Bread tin – Only necessary if you like making bread
Chopping board – Many yachts have some form of chopping board
  incorporated into the galley, usually as a cover to the sink
Cling film
Colander
Corkscrews
Drying-up cloths
Dustpan and brush
Egg poacher – It is possible to buy one that fits inside a saucepan
  or frying pan
Egg timer – More useful for waking the skipper in time for the
  weather forecast
Fire blanket – Should be kept in the galley within easy reach
Fire extinguisher
Fish slice
Flint lighter – For the stove
Frying pan – Essential, despite the wagging fingers from the health-
  conscious warning us about the perils of fried food, there is no
  quicker way to cheer the crew up after a cold and miserable night
  watch than the aroma of frying bacon
Graduated measuring jug – Used for liquid and dry ingredients
Grater
Grill pan
Heat diffuser – Handy for keeping pots simmering gently at a very
  low heat
Kitchen cleaner
Kitchen paper
Knives – 1 large, 1 small and 1 with a serrated edge for cutting
  bread. Protect the points by sticking them into a cork. I also
  keep one old broken knife which is used for cutting rope, cleaning
  some part of the engine or even as a screwdriver
Lavatory brush
Lavatory cleaner
Lavatory paper – Overestimation of the amount to take never
  matters
Lighter – For cigars and cigarettes as well as stove lighting

Matches – As a back-up for the flint lighter, kept in a waterproof container – also consider waterproof matches for emergencies

Oven gloves – Gauntlet type

Ovenproof dishes

Potato peeler

Pressure cooker – This single item of equipment has done for sea-going cooks what the microwave oven did for restaurateurs. On several races it has been the only saucepan I have had on board. Even if it does fall off the cooker, as long as the lid is on, your dinner will not land up in the bilges, or over the cook. Neither will you find yourself having to navigate your way round a deposit of baked beans instead of the Isle of Wight. It saves on fuel and time; meals can be prepared in advance and left-overs added for the next day or two. In hot weather and without a fridge, providing the food is brought to pressure for three minutes and then left to cool and the seal is *not* broken or the weight removed, the contents will keep for two or three days. It is possible to buy a small cooker that holds enough for two people as well as larger sizes. Automatic release valves save the trouble of having to douse the whole pan in a bucket of water when you need to release the pressure. There is a model that has an automatic timer on the top, which is very good in theory. In practice, when the cooker has been thrown off the stove to the floor a couple of times, the timer breaks. There is an Italian make that has a lid that doubles as an ordinary lid, or can be clamped and used as a pressure cooker. It is made of high quality stainless steel, is heavy and extremely expensive

Rolling pin – A clean wine bottle will do just as well

Saucepans – If space allows, then three different sizes are very convenient. Non-stick pans get scratched. Protect the surface by stowing them with a lining of kitchen towel. If you are an inveterate porridge eater, then one non-stick pan is essential. It is also invaluable for scrambled eggs. If space is at a premium, one large and one small are sufficient

Scissors – Kitchen type. There should be a separate pair for medical purposes only, kept in the first-aid box

Slotted draining spoon

Soup ladle

Sponges – Better to take too many than too few and find that
someone uses your best floor one for mopping up spilt diesel

Strainer

Tin-opener – One for everyday use and several hidden away in
case of emergency. Like small electrical screwdrivers and
foredeck hands, they are never around when you need them

Washing-up brush

Washing-up liquid

Whisk – Only if you think you might be making meringues or
whipping cream. Some people use them for making omelettes,
but a fork will do. Rotating ones rust up in no time at all; an
ordinary hand one is best

Wooden spoon(s)

CHAPTER THREE

Planning the Victuals

The most disagreeable thing at sea is the cookery; for there is not, properly speaking, any professional cook on board. The worst sailor is generally chosen for that purpose. Hence comes the proverb used among the English sailors, that 'God sends meat, and the Devil sends cooks'.

Benjamin Franklin, 'Precautions to be Used by
Those who are About to Undertake a Sea Voyage'

When we first started cruising our diet was simple. It seldom varied from bully beef or pilchards in tomato sauce for lunch and tinned stew and fresh vegetables for dinner. It was not from any parsimony on the part of the skipper, merely the limited range of tinned food available twenty-five years ago. We spent several seasons cruising the west coast of Scotland and Ireland as well as the north-west coast of Spain, where the majority of our anchorages were usually far from habitation, the closest village with a shop and, more important, a pub, often being on the other side of a hill. A vigorous tramp across moors and bog works up a legitimate thirst. I remember once making a phone call from the only public box for fifty miles and the lady who worked the exchange asking me if I would be kind enough to relay various messages around the village (not everyone had a telephone). One of the messages was for a crofter's wife to tell her that her niece's baby had been born that morning. Message duly delivered, we all repaired to the pub where the landlord boasted thirty-four different brands of malt whisky: I remember only seventeen.

Then, few – if any – yachts were fitted with a cold-box, let alone a fridge or deep-freeze. Cruising in an area where the population was sparse meant that most of our stores were bought at the beginning of the season. The only shopping we did was for fresh bread and vegetables. We relied on ingenuity and imagination to vary our diet. The novice galley-slave had been given some useful advice on how to hoodwink the crew into thinking that dinner would be a gastronomic experience and not the inevitable pot mess stew. All you had to do was to heat some butter or oil in a frying pan, gently sauté a clove or two of garlic and as soon as the pungent aroma of that bulb began to permeate the cockpit, those up on watch would sniff the air like Bisto kids in anticipation of a mouth-watering feast to come; meanwhile down in the galley tins of this and that were being opened and mixed together with the frequent slurp of wine.

The worst meal I have ever served up was at Plockton on the west coast of Scotland where we had been gale-bound for a couple of days. I think that I was trying to impress some chap or other and felt that a little culinary excitement was called for. Leafing through our recipe book, I decided on a steamed ginger pudding. This called for a pudding basin which we did not have, so when I mentioned what I intended to cook for supper the young man's eyes lit up and he even offered to row me ashore to the village to buy a suitable pot. Pot purchased, I set to with a will and after hours of bubbling and hissing this mouth-watering wonder was finally ready to serve. It took a great deal of shaking and pounding to turn it out and almost as much effort to extract the accompanying sauce from the pan. It was eaten in almost total silence. That pudding still lies as heavily on my conscience as it did on our stomachs.

When planning for a cruise of more than a week you will need to stock up with enough tins and general provisions, so that the only shopping you will have to do during the voyage will be for essential fresh food. Personally, I feel that as it is my holiday too, shopping every day is the last thing I intend doing. You should also take into account that, although you anticipate the longest passage to be only two to three days, the wise virgin makes allowance for that well-known phenomenon, Sod's Law, which means you will almost certainly be at sea for longer than you think. If you plan your menus on the basis of having three meals a day, you will end up with more than enough supplies, as in reality there are plenty of days when for one reason or another you may not eat three full meals.

The most important part of meal planning is to build as much variety as you can into your menus – there is nothing worse than having to eat bully beef in one form or another for six days, let alone six months. Let us suppose that you are planning a six-month cruise to the West Indies. Should you take tinned and dried supplies for the whole six months? The logistics of this pose a bit of a conundrum as there are at least three things to consider. First of all weight: the heavier your boat is the slower you will go, therefore longer time on passage requires more supplies. Second, climate: you must take into consideration any change in climate and adjust your eating habits accordingly. Will you want to eat plates of porridge or steak and kidney pudding under a blazing tropical sun in English Harbour or lick ice lollies as you round the North Cape? Third, on small islands in particular where the local community live on or below subsistence level, they cannot be blamed for charging visitors enormous sums of money for the fruit and vegetables that they can grow. For example, in the West Indies you may find yourself paying as much as fifty pence for one tomato. On islands anywhere most of the food is imported and consequently expensive, so you may well be forced to eat some of your supplies. It is worth checking the prices of the local restaurants in the West Indies: it may be cheaper to eat out than to buy fresh food. Remember, too, that it is pointless trying to buy bacon produce in a country or island that has never seen a pig. My advice to those planning this sort of cruise would be to break it into three sections: the passage out, time spent cruising, and the the return voyage.

REFRIGERATION

A small, custom-designed fridge draws the minimum of 50 amp/hrs daily in the tropics and a typical stock model can easily consume between 120 – 145 amp/hrs a day. If your fridge runs off an engine-driven compressor pump, this means you would need to run the engine for at least two to three hours a day. Deep-freezes are even more power hungry. Those who have spent a lot of time cruising in hot climates would say that a fridge is not a luxury and that a one-and-a-half-to-two cubic foot fridge is adequate. The key to a successful fridge is insulation. Some manufacturers of fridges frequently installed in caravans and yachts don't really know how to cope with the tropics. If you are departing for the tropics and decide to fit a fridge, keep the box itself small and have more room for packing insulation around the outside. This will mean increased efficiency and less time spent with the engine thumping away shattering the peace in an anchorage in paradise.

If your yacht has a deep-freeze, when you enter a new port find out from charter boats where they do their shopping, because you can be sure that they know the cheapest and the most reliable sources. On the small islands the ferry brings frozen food from the larger islands or the mainland and it is highly likely that food may have been thawed and refrozen several times before it gets to you.

It is dangerous to rely on the deep-freeze as the only means of storage. There are numerous tales of woe from yachtsmen who have been caught out having stocked up their deep-freezes with mountains of food and little else only to find the hitherto trusty engine dies or a gremlin has got into the generator – there has been no remedy but to eat solidly for two days and then throw the rest away. If you do not have a fridge, there are two easy ways of cooling wine. In north European waters the sea temperature is fairly stable about five feet down, so a bottle suspended on a length of string over the side is one way of cooling it. In hotter climates, stand the bottle in a bucket with about three inches of water, cover with a wet cloth and place where there is the most breeze; the cooling process works through evaporation.

Food poisoning can be avoided by being sensible. Refrozen poultry is one hazard, while in some countries the local water supply may be dubious. Ask around and if in doubt buy bottled water. It is more often than not the pipes or hose connected to the tap or the collecting tank that are contaminated rather than the source of the water. When we sailed in Turkey we replenished our tanks once from a spring on a beach which had, according to the locals, been there for generations, maybe even a couple of thousand years. It was beautiful.

Half the fun of cruising in foreign countries is wandering around the markets and trying out some of the local fruit and vegetables. The tiresome part is carting it all back aboard. In the Mediterranean and the tropics *never* take cardboard cartons, carrier bags or boxes back on board – unless you want to run the risk of infesting your boat with cockroaches or other creepy-crawlies. Once on board cockroaches are impossible to get rid of. A cardboard box may look quite innocent, but cockroach eggs are microscopic, and you can bet that any box that has been lying around in a shop is heavily infected. Cockroaches are the most invasive insects – you rarely see them during the day, but you know that behind every locker door, under every dark corner they are there, and at night out come the antennae-waving fiends to plague you. Every poison, bomb and spray known to man cannot kill them. They say that even after a full-scale nuclear war the only creature to survive will be the cockroach. Ants are another pest: they love to nestle inside hands of bananas.

Rats are still a problem in various parts of the world and you still see ships with anti-rat guards, a circle of metal on their mooring warps; this discourages all but the most determined of rats. Two very good friends of ours lived with an Egyptian rat for months. It climbed aboard at Ismailia on their way through the Suez canal *en route* for Dubai and lived on a shocking diet consisting mainly of the plastic covering of electrical wiring cables. It sulked in the bilges by day, and at night Rachael would wake up to see its whiskers silhouetted against the moon. They tried everything to get rid of it: poisoned cheese, lying in wait with winch handle at the ready, even Mogadon sandwiches hoping to send it to sleep, but like all of his kind he skilfully evaded their efforts and continued to munch happily away to the detriment of their electrics. When they finally reached Dubai the rat met his end at the hands of the municipal Arab rat-catcher.

STORES

There is nothing worse than the thought of running out of food when you are far from land and can do nothing about it. Most people, myself included, usually overestimate the quantity needed for the trip so the problem is unlikely to arise. But it can happen as it did to one skipper I know who had a very successful one-tonner. On this type of yacht, weight is critical and extra stores and gear were kept to a minimum. Each week the crew took it in turns to supply the food for the weekend race, a casual system that had worked well all season. They set off on a Channel Race late Friday afternoon with a reasonable start. Once clear of the Needles, the wind freed them sufficiently to set the spinnaker and they began to overtake the leaders; morale was high and the skipper thought that they might as well take advantage of the situation and have supper before settling down to the night watches. The crew nodded their agreement, but no one made a move towards the galley.

'Fred, wasn't it your turn to do supper?' asked the skipper. 'Er no, it's Bert's turn isn't it?' Bert looked equally blank. Pockets and kitbags were turned out and the net contents consisted of one packet of sandwiches, half a bar of chocolate and a couple of apples. Apart from water there was nothing else on board. Luckily it was a fairly short race, 150 miles or so, which they won in record time – perhaps gorillas work harder on empty stomachs, but I don't think I should dare put it to the test.

Most cruising yachtsmen do not have to worry about too much excess weight and carry sufficient stores on board to last all season. It is a matter of individual choice as to whether you prefer to cater for each weekend at a time, or whether you prefer to keep a basic supply on board which you supplement with fresh bread and milk, etc. We usually compromise by bringing one or maybe two pre-cooked meals with us. Whichever way you choose to organize your catering, it always pays to carry sufficient tins or packets of pasta and rice on board for emergencies, such as when the children turn up with a troop of starving friends. Here are a few suggestions for provisions with notes on which items keep better than others.

Bacon – Unopened vacuum-packed bacon keeps well, even after its 'use by' date. Keep them where the packets will not be damaged and in as cool a place as possible, the bilges for example. Should the packet be damaged it will bulge and must be thrown away.

Bovril – Hot drinks or as a spread.

Bread – Wholemeal, wholewheat, granary, white or brown, sliced, fresh, frozen or half-baked? The choice seems endless. But what we are interested in is which kind of bread keeps the longest. There are several solutions to this problem. If you have an oven, and few yachts these days are without, then the 'half-baked' variety is a useful and delicious stand-by. Its disadvantage is that it does have a limited shelf-life, which makes it unsuitable to keep as a stand-by for more than about a month. It is usually available as small French-type loaves and one stick will not go far as the crew usually attack fresh bread like a host of gannets. There is a type of long-life bread which can be found in some health food shops. One type is made of rye and one with sprouted grain. There is also a gluten-free variety for those who may not be able to eat ordinary bread. They all taste rather sour; even heating them in the oven or under the grill does little to improve them. They are, to my way of thinking, an acquired taste. Pumpernickel is preferable and has a long shelf-life. You can always make your own bread, but many people feel there is too much effort involved. If you do, then take a tip from the long-distance cruising fraternity who recommend carrying tubs of whole wheat which they grind on board to make their bread, as they find that ordinary flour is more prone to weevil infestation, especially in remote parts of the world.

Ordinary sliced bread does keep reasonably well for at least two weeks if kept cool and dry, although you may find a bit of mould towards the end of the third week. The worst thing you can do to bread of any kind is to freeze it, unless of course you have a deep-freeze on board and intend to keep it frozen; once frozen and allowed to thaw it goes stale very much quicker. As a final resort there are always the Ryvita-type biscuits and the French biscottes which, if kept unopened in a plastic box, will last for months, are nice and crunchy and make a welcome change every so often.

Butter – Salted butter keeps well without refrigeration, in our climate at least, for a month before turning rancid. With no deep-freeze or fridge, wrap the butter in tinfoil and stow it in the bilges where it should keep for at least a couple of months. Tinned butter will keep almost indefinitely.

Cereals – Our favourite is a home-made muesli. Store all cereals in plastic containers. Packets of breakfast cereal, Shreddies and the like, go stale once opened unless eaten within a week or two.

Cheese – 'A meal without a cheese is like a beautiful woman with only one eye' (Brillat-Savarin).

Hard cheese lasts well, notably English Cheddars or Double Gloucester, which are now sold in some of the big supermarkets as 5lb truckles rather than the familiar giant cartwheels all year round. The beauty of taking a whole cheese with you on an ocean voyage is its lasting qualities. Small slices of cheese, 1–2lb pieces, will keep for a week or two provided they are not kept in a plastic box where they will sweat and grow mould. I know of Cheddar cheeses that have sailed from England to Cape Town via America. *En route* the cheese had been through a variety of temperature changes and still remained in good condition. Slice off the top and use it as a 'lid'. Peel down the outer cloth as you eat the cheese and fold it back over the cheese as you use it up. One of the delights of France is the enormous choice of cheese

open to you. They say that there are 365 different varieties, one
for each day of the year, but where the cheese is required to last,
stick to the hard type. 'Appericubes' are small cubes of cheese
in assorted flavours. They are made by a French company that
makes processed cheese and can be found in this country – very
good with the evening tot. These will keep for a week or two
provided they are not kept in a plastic box to sweat and grow
mould. A container of grated Parmesan is well worth having to
sprinkle over pasta dishes.

Cocoa – Or chocolate powder for hot drinks.

Coffee – Individual sachets are lighter and keep their flavour better
for a long time. Real ground coffee lasts well in plastic containers.

Croutons – Packets of herb- or garlic-flavoured croutons are
delicious in salads and in omelettes.

Dried potato – Very useful as a stand-by vegetable on its own and
can also be used with great effect to thicken stews or soups.

Eggs – Providing these have not been refrigerated or chilled they
will keep for months. We are lucky in this country as they are
not stored in this fashion. In other parts of the world, notably
North America, they may have been chilled, in which case they
last for only about two weeks. If you are taking them for a long
voyage of more than a month, remember to turn them over at
least once a week to prevent the yolk settling at one end and
consequently leaking out of the shell. There is no need to go to
the trouble smearing them with Vaseline. Dried egg powder should
be carried for emergencies.

Flour – Unless you anticipate making bread, a small amount for
making a sauce comes in handy. Cornflour is useful to thicken
sauces as well as making custard.

French dressing – Have a jar ready made on hand as it saves time.

Garlic – I have never found the dried garlic granules satisfactory.
Fresh bulbs of garlic keep for weeks (a cool dark place is best).
Some people like to use a garlic crusher, but I find them a nuisance
to clean. Crushing a clove with the flat side of a knife is just as
effective.

Herbs – Jars of dried herbs and spices, such as mixed Provençal
herbs, bay leaves, cumin, coriander and cardamom, curry powder
and mixed spice. Owners of large and stable yachts can find room

to grow their own fresh herbs. Empty 35mm film cases are good for small amounts.

Honey – Delicious with bread and butter and also as a sweetener in drinks.

Jam – Marmalade, jam, or whichever is your favourite spread.

Margarine – There are several different types of margarine available, including those made from saturated or unsaturated fats. There are also low-fat spreads for the diet-conscious. If you are on a special diet it is always advisable to take your own preferred spread with you in case it is not available where you are going. The disadvantage of the easy-spreading brands is that they do not keep in hot climates unless in fridge.

Marmite – Useful for drinks as well as a spread.

Mayonnaise – Jars of real mayonnaise will not last for more than a couple of weeks once they have been opened. Tubes of the same thing keep much better.

Milk – Fresh milk will keep a few days in the fridge, longlife, once opened, a little longer. Longlife milk is difficult to find in many countries including America, so take enough with you unless you are sure you will find it where you are going. Keep it for passages as in a hot climate is goes off very quickly. Dried milk is essential as a stand-by as well as for making Yorkshire pudding – it makes a wonderfully light batter and can be bought in individual sachets.

Mustard – A tube of Colman's English mustard as well as a jar of French or German mustard.

Nuts – Tins of dry-roasted peanuts, smoky salted almonds, cashew and pistachio nuts. Walnuts are good in salads. If any of the nuts begin to taste stale, refresh them by heating in the oven for a few minutes.

Oil – For salads and frying.

Pasta – A packet of pasta (hard variety, not fresh) with a sauce is an excellent stand-by. An unopened packet will last the season. Different shapes, bows and spirals, for example, are good eaten cold mixed into a salad of raw vegetables.

Peanut Butter – This is something that people either love or hate. It is highly nutritious and can be used in a number of different ways. As a sauce with skewers of grilled chicken, or with jam in sandwiches.

Pepper – Pepper mills will jam unless the mill part is made of plastic. Ground pepper is a simpler alternative.

Pickles – Chutney etc.

Pudding mix – There are numbers of dessert mixes which require only mixing with milk to make an instant pudding. Some, like a caramel flavour, are quite nice as a change; on the whole they are more popular with junior crew members. Crumble mixes for the top of the fruit pies are well worth taking.

Rice – Basmati is by far the nicest rice; it has a delicate flavour all of its own and is delicious plain or in a risotto. It can be kept in the packet or plastic container. If sailing two-handed or alone, divide bags into 2–4oz (30–60g) plastic bags.

Salt – Is hygroscopic. Some people recommend putting grains of rice in the pot to stop it going solid, but on a boat you may as well not bother. I buy salt in a plastic container so that when it turns into a solid block it is easy to separate again by tapping it gently. Salt mills are useless on board.

Sauces – Only in the last few years have jars of Pesto (basil), Crema di Oliva (olive paste) and Crema di Pomodoro (dried tomato paste), appeared on supermarket shelves. A spoonful or two stirred into a bowl of cooked pasta with a dusting of grated Parmesan on top makes a brilliant meal on its own. There are also good instant packet sauces such as bread, apple, onion and quite a few other flavours; it is certainly worth having a few on board, plus soy sauce to give an exotic flavour to stir-fried vegetables and chicken.

Soup (packets) – Where should we be without Cup-a-Soups? The type with *croutons* is my favourite.

Stock cubes – They also come in a variety of flavours as well as vegetarian.

Sugar – Brown or white.

Tea – China and Indian as well as other exotic brands come in bags.

Tinned sauces – Varieties of tomato-based sauce to add to pasta: Bolognese, mushroom and herbs, etc.

Vinegar – Wine vinegar for salad dressing.

Yoghurt – Look out for long-life yoghurt in supermarkets.

TINS AND VACUUM-PACKED FOODS

Tins of food will keep for years providing they do not rust due to being exposed to salt water. At the end of the sailing season it is advisable to remove *everything* from the lockers and wash them out thoroughly with fresh water. A marina berth has the obvious advantage in that there is usually a supply of fresh water and a hose to make the job a lot easier. A hot-air blower fire will make the drying-out process very much quicker. If planning a voyage of several months it is advisable to remove the labels from the tins and label them with an indelible marker. I know that I am not alone in finding that the tin of chilli-con-carne I was looking forward to for supper turned out to be custard. It is surprisingly easy for labels to come unstuck even if your lockers are dry, and if your lockers are not, there is nothing that will jam up a bilge pump quicker than soggy paper labels. Should this happen, the only cure is to dismantle the pump and remove the blockage; this is not a popular task in the confines of a small boat pitching about in the dark – in my experience nearly all disasters occur at night. Long-distance cruising people recommend that it is worth all the hard work involved to varnish the tins as well.

Vacuum-packed smoked chicken and turkey are delicious hot or cold, but once opened will not keep for more than a day or two. Unopened they have quite a long shelf-life, but by no means indefinite. Search the shelves for the longest 'sell-by' date. Vacuum-packed turkey legs are good hot or cold.

Bottled foods

I have heard about the delicious meat that some cruising people, especially in the States, have bottled at home. But I have it on good authority that this practice could be dangerous and is not recommended because there is a high risk of food poisoning. Meat must be cooked at a very high temperature before it is completely sterilized and bacteria destroyed. This is only possible in a pressure cooker and the length of cooking time involved means that the meat will have been broken down much the same as it is in tins. I am wary of taking many glass jars as there is always the danger of breakages. If you do, make sure they are securely packed.

Tins

The following are a few of the tins that I find the most useful as they form the basis of so many different types of meal. Everyone has favourites and this list may jog your memory or give you an idea or two.

Artichoke – Hearts or bottoms, can be used in a number of different ways.

Beans – Baked beans in tomato sauce. Red kidney beans which are good fillers when added to stews or cold in salads. Butter and French green flageolets are nice with raw onions and tuna, and can also be added to stews; flageolets are especially good heated up with the juice from roast lamb.

Beef, corned – Sometimes called bully beef. It is extremely versatile as it can be eaten straight from the tin or cooked in a number of different ways. Very good in stews as it does not go mushy.

Boil-in-box or bag meals – There is a wide range of tasty meals that are heated by boiling in water for 10 minutes.

Chick peas – Delicious with a spicy tomato sauce, added to stews or mashed up with garlic and lemon juice as hummus.

Chilli-con-carne – Basis of an instant meal.

Condensed milk – Simmer a tin for at least an hour to make caramel sauce. Take great care when opening the tin. Delicious with ice-cream.

Frankfurters – Tasty fried or in hot-dogs and chopped into soups, also good cold chopped into salad with walnuts, celery and cold potatoes.

Fruit – As wide a variety as possible. Luckily the demand for sugar-free food means that there are more varieties of unsweetened tinned fruit on the market. Tinned plums are very good in a crumble or with custard.

Ham – Tinned is quite good as a stand-by, but beware of jelly liquefying in hot climates.

Ham & pork, chopped – Cheaper alternative to ham and can be sliced and fried.

Hot cans/meals – Self-heating cans are good to have in an emergency.

Mince – This is better value than stews which tend to be rather watery and the meat mushy in texture. Plain mince is better value than the kind with added vegetables.

Mincemeat – Sometimes popular when sailing in cool climates. Add a little whisky to make a superior mince pie.

Mushrooms – They are quite expensive so I buy only one or two for special occasions. Good in omelettes.

Pâté – A wide range of assorted pâtés, made of game, liver and fish.

Potatoes – A few tinned new ones for special occasions.

Ratatouille – Good hot or cold and mixed with eggs as a quiche.

Sardines – Nice hot or cold with the added benefit that they are highly nutritious. French supermarkets sell sardines in various sauces which are delicious.

Soups – It is worth taking a few tins of condensed soup, as they are useful in sauces, also a few tins of special soups like crab, lobster, venison or game for special occasions.

Spinach – Puréed it is fairly sloppy on its own, but makes a good soup with added stock cube and water. Excellent when added to mashed potatoes.

Sweetcorn – The American white corn has the sweetest flavour.

Tomatoes – Whole or crushed Italian tomatoes are essential for adding to any kind of stew made from fresh or tinned meat. Also excellent in any bean-based dishes. They contain a higher amount of vitamin C than most other tinned vegetables.

Tuna – Even more versatile than bully beef. Tuna mayonnaise, salad Niçoise, fish pie, kedgeree, with beans.

DRIED FOOD

Beans – Kidney, black (not available in this country in tins) and butter beans, chick peas. More economical than tinned, but need cooking – I recommend dried pulses when cruising, tinned for racing.

Dried meals – Numerous varieties, good if you are short of space or weight is critical, and quite handy for padding out tinned or fresh meals. In the States there is a range of freeze-dried meals made by Mountain House which are found in stores that cater for hikers and campers. Their flavour is excellent. Connie van Rietschoten used them aboard *Flyer* during both the Whitbread Round the World races.

Dried mixed veg – Useful as a standby for flavouring or if you are short of space or weight-conscious.

Dried noodles – If you are in a hurry they are simple to prepare and can be made and eaten from a large mug.

Dried peas – Reconstituted they are very good on their own and by far the best of the dried vegetables.

Dried potato – Smash is excellent on its own or can be used with great effect to thicken stews.

Dried yeast – Keeps fresh for about six months but no longer.

Lentils – Red lentils require very little cooking. Good in soups, stews or with any Indian-type meal.

Meat – Biltong is the name given to the notorious wind-dried strips of game from South Africa; Biltong Bertie Reed, of the same country, was given this nickname as a tribute to his innate toughness.

Noodles – Packets of Chinese noodles are quite handy as they are light and take up very little room. They need softening in a mug of hot water for only 4 minutes to provide a quick instant meal.

Pasta – Keeps well and forms the basis of many different hot dishes, or cold as a salad.

Salami – Keep one or more hanging up. The crew love hacking off a slice to eat with the evening noggin. If the salami begin to sweat in warm weather, transfer them to the rigging to dry.

Smoked ham – A pig's hind leg swinging in the rigging has a certain piratical look about it. Several well-known yachtsmen never leave port without one.

Vegetables – Onions, peas, peppers and mushrooms are all good when rehydrated.

FRESH FOODS

In the USA and some European countries, fresh and some frozen foods are treated by irradiation to preserve them. Of course, the moment it was announced that all of Europe was intending to use this method of preservation, some people began to wonder what it was all about. If we ate irradiated food, some suggested, we should glow in the dark. Simply, food irradiation is a physical means of food treatment comparable to processing food by heating or freezing it. The process involves exposing food, either prepackaged or in bulk, to gamma rays,

X-rays or electrons, in a special room and for a specified duration. In a sense, exposing food to gamma radiation is similar to exposing it to electric light: such exposure, for no matter how long, will never cause the food to generate electricity. It is safer as well as more efficient and cheaper than spraying crops with pesticides and fungicides. Fresh food is exposed to low levels of gamma irradiation to lengthen its shelf-life. Other practical uses of irradiation include inhibiting the sprouting of onions and potatoes during storage, to control insect infestation in dried dates and spices and to extend shelf-life and eliminate pathogenic micro-organisms in meat and fish.

Fruit – Fresh fruit such as apples, oranges, grapefruit, pineapples, bananas and avocados will keep well if bought when unripe and kept in a cool dark place where the air can circulate. This is where nets come in useful for stowage. Most fruit brought from supermarkets has been kept in an artificially cool environment. Once it is brought into a normal temperature it will ripen quickly. If at all possible buy your fruit and vegetables from a 'pick-your-own' farm. Soft fruit will not keep for long. This includes fruit such as pears, peaches and plums, as well as the berry fruits such as strawberries, raspberries and blueberries. Keep all of this kind of fruit separately so that if mould develops before you notice, they will not infect the rest of your fruit supply.

Melons – A great favourite with everyone. The highly-scented varieties such as cantaloupe should be kept separate if possible, as they can taint some other foods including milk, for example. The same applies to other strong-smelling fruit such as guavas and mangoes. Water melons keep well and are refreshing on a hot day.

Vegetables – The hard cabbages that look like green cannon balls will keep for weeks. They are best for shredding to make cole-slaw. Like fruit, all the hard vegetables keep well but remove them from any plastic wrapping. Loose-leafed green vegetables will only keep for a short time, usually not more than a week. Broccoli, cauliflower and Brussels sprouts keep longer than runner or haricot (French) beans. Remember that soft vegetables have a high water content and any fruit or vegetable with a soft outer skin will decompose quickly. Courgettes rot quicker than the type of marrow or squash that has a tough outer skin.

Salads – Hard-packed lettuce like iceberg and Webb keep better than the softer varieties. Cucumbers keep quite well as long as they are not kept in the normal plastic wrapping. Make a point of buying tomatoes at different stages of ripeness to ensure a long supply. Chinese leaves, fennel and radishes all enliven salads.

Bean Sprouts – Several different sprouting beans can be grown very easily on board and they make a welcome addition to salads and are very nutritious. They are best eaten raw but can be stir-fried, added to omelettes, sprinkled on the top of soup or put in sandwiches.

Aduki – Slower growing than the others and slightly more expensive.

Alfalfa – Fastest growing and will grow 14mm in two days in a warm environment. Personally I like these the best.

Mung – Take three to five days to grow. Nice, slightly nutty taste and excellent stir-fried.

Mustard and cress – Both good grown beyond the sprouting stage to leaf stage, good in sandwiches. Francis Chichester and Bill King both grew these when they sailed round the world.

Soya – Strong flavour. Best stir-fried.

Wheat – A little goes a long way, but worth trying.

Sprouting

You will need large wide-necked jars, (at home I use a glass jar, but at sea it is safer to use large plastic tonic or soda bottles with the tops cut off, which are lighter in weight too), a piece of muslin or the toe of an old pair of tights or stockings, a rubber band. Put one or two tablespoons of seeds into a jar, being careful not to put in too many. Stretch the stocking over the top of the jar and secure it with an elastic band. Pour through enough warm water to cover the seeds easily and leave overnight in a warm place. In the morning, drain off the water through the cloth and rinse with a little fresh water. Drain again and turn the jar upside down so that the water continues to drain off. Seeds left in water will not sprout. Rinse out every morning for two or three days, or until ready to eat.

Meat

Poultry and pork should not be kept for any length of time without refrigeration. In warm weather they may begin to smell high even after a day. As long as the smell is not too strong, and the meat not discoloured, wash it in a solution of water and vinegar before cooking. If in any doubt at all, throw it away. Red meat will last longer and can also benefit from being kept in a marinade for a few days, providing you are sailing in a cool climate. Salt beef keeps in its brine for months – delicious.

When on passage for more than a couple of days, the evening meal assumes an importance all of its own. It is the social highlight, as it is often the only time of the day that the whole crew get together. Except on the most disciplined of yachts competing in long-distance races, the 'happy' hour pre-supper is the one time of the day when the crew can unwind and take the opportunity of the informal atmosphere to air any minor grievances in a lighthearted fashion; when sailing two-handed, the steering committee meet with the board of navigation and settle any differences of opinion over dinner.

When planning your stores list try to ensure that no meal is repeated in under a week. To do this you have to be imaginative as well as organized. By all means get inspiration from cookery books and supermarket shelves, then sit down and make a list. To make the diet interesting, think of planning to have a meal from a different country each night. For example – Italian: pasta shells, tortellini, spaghetti; French: a stew made with a red wine sauce, anything Provençal with onions, tomatoes and garlic, fish with a mushroom and white wine sauce, lamb with haricot beans; Indian: curry with meat or vegetables, spicy or hot to taste; English: shepherd's pie, fish pie, ham with parsley sauce, boiled salt beef and carrots; Chinese: stir-fried meat and vegetables, noodles, bean sprouts and spare ribs; American: hamburgers, ham with pineapple and barbecued flavoured anything. Then there are what I would loosely term as 'mongrel foreign', such as chilli-con-carne and sweet-'n'-sour sauces that drown the taste of slightly high meat. Beware!

If planning to take young children with you on any protracted trip you will need to cater for their tastes, too; anyone who has sailed with children will know just how capricious the little darlings' tastes can be. You think that you have loaded all their favourite snacks on board when suddenly in the middle of the North Sea comes a demand for a peanut butter sandwich. The floodgates open when you remind them that there is none on board because they said only last week that it was 'yukky and revolting'. The same is true if you have bought up the entire stock of Sainsbury's baked beans with hot dogs as it was the one thing that your child would eat, only to find that three days out they were demanding bacon sandwiches and flatly refused to look at a plate of beans.

EMERGENCY STORES

Somewhere on board there should be a secret place for emergency stores. This is not just iron rations in case of shipwreck, but special treats like birthdays. There are always those moments when it is 'time for a little something', as that remarkable Bear of Very Little Brain once said. I am a great believer in treats for the high or low points of a long passage. In particular, when ocean crossing, little presents to celebrate special occasions like reaching the half-way point are always appreciated. We sent one friend off with enough Bendicks bittermints, his one addiction, so that he could have one a day for six weeks. You could also include a few paper hats, whistles and party-popper streamers for any festive occasion.

WATER

Apart from your main water tanks, it is a wise precaution to carry at least 2 gallons of water in separate containers in case of emergency. A competitor in a race to the Azores thought for a moment that his boat was sinking when he awoke to the sound of water slopping around the cabin sole. In spite of looking everywhere for signs of damage to the hull, he could not find where the water was coming from. He then realized that his one polythene water tank had burst. He had only a gallon of water left in a separate container. In fact he never really went short as he had plenty of fruit juice as well as water in tinned vegetables and was also able to catch some rain-water. A conservative way to calculate the amount of water to take with you is to use the time-honoured formula of 2 pints per person per day. This calculation does not take into consideration the amount of water needed if there are those on board who insist on washing their hair only in fresh water. Apart from your main tanks leaking, there is the possibility that they could get contaminated. In the event of having to take to your liferaft, it is sensible to fill your spare water containers only three-quarters full so that they float. Remember that dehydration kills quicker than starvation.

THE PANIC BAG

A panic bag to take with you into the life raft should be kept within easy reach of the cockpit; each member of the crew must know where it is kept. It should at least contain: some white hand-held, and red parachute flares and an orange smoke flare, an EPIRB, and/or a hand-held VHF, torch, knife, glucose tablets, seasick pills and bottled water as well as some dry clothes or a dry suit. We use a flare canister for a panic bag as it is a convenient size and waterproof. At one time, many people thought that a space blanket, designed to prevent loss of body heat, a sensible thing to take. In practice, so I am told by someone who has tried one out in anger, they are difficult to keep wrapped around and it has been suggested that large, tough polythene bags of the type used for fertilizer are better, as they can keep you dry and, more important, protect you from the windchill factor. For ocean cruising a more comprehensive panic bag might include a device for catching rainwater, a desalination gadget that uses the heat from the sun to distil sea water, a first aid box, fishing tackle, 'compo' rations, a Swiss army knife, sextant, routing chart and pencils.

CHAPTER FOUR

Estimating Consumable Stores

In the late eighteenth century, a sailor's provisions consisted of 1lb of hard biscuit, 1 gallon of beer, dried peas, oatmeal or flour daily, 2lb of salt beef and 2lb of pork twice a week, 8oz of butter and 12oz of cheese a week. In those days the victualling board was concerned with quantity rather than quality. Like the army which marches on its stomach, sailors put up with appalling conditions of shipboard life only if well fed. A surprising number of mutinies were caused by lack of proper food rather than for any other reason. Much of the food was inedible at the time of issue – butter and cheese rancid within a week, pork available only if live pigs were on hand for slaughter.

DAY SAILING AND RACES

Catering for a day's race should not present any problems. But if the owner's wife has never put food on board her husband's day-racing machine, she may find it extraordinarily difficult to understand the feeding requirements of his team of gorillas unless properly briefed. It would be a waste of her time and energy if piles of bridge rolls, quiche and salad ended up in the gash bin when a Mars bar and an apple would have been sufficient. In any case, most day races end before the bar closes. Setting out for a relaxed day's sail can mean taking anything from a packet of sandwiches and a slab of fruit cake to a full-scale hamper from Harrods. Whatever you do, don't forget to take the picnic out of the back of the car.

WEEKENDS

The weekend on board the boat away from all the hustle and bustle of city life is still Everyman's way of recharging his batteries for the week ahead. In the old days this was probably the only time a chap went anywhere near a cooker or tin-opener. To that generation of sailors, the whole concept of yachting was much more of a Gung-Ho, Scout activity. Part of the fun was being cold, wet and miserable, while being warm and comfortable was considered a bit soft. Likewise, opening a can of baked beans for supper was perfectly in keeping with the general sense of adventure. The 'adventure' is still there all right, like discovering the Decca has gone on the blink and you don't know where you are, but instead of opening the proverbial baked beans, you open a foil packet of gourmet duck *à l'orange*. The variety of ready-made meals sold in the major supermarkets are delicious enough to be served up at the smartest London dinner parties, and the garlicky aroma of chicken Kiev wafts from any number of galleys on a Saturday night. It may be an extravagant way of catering for the weekend but it is very convenient.

The racing crew over a weekend is simple enough to plan for and can be tackled two ways. Either the crew provide their own sandwiches with the owner's wife providing a ready-to-heat-and-eat supper; or she may provide the crew with everything. Don't forget that at lunch-time, a busy crew will not have time to fiddle about with knives and forks or salads that spill everywhere leaving lethal deposits of slippery oil on the cockpit sole. Neither would the helmsman, fighting the wheel on a shy spinnaker reach, be exactly thrilled should you hand him a red-hot baked potato. Food should be kept as simple as possible. What sailors require is food that can be held easily in one hand and that won't fall to pieces: a meal in a bun. Soft drinks in cans, or individual fruit drinks with a straw are easier to cope with than mugs or flimsy paper cups. The serious owner will probably insist on paper plates to save the weight of proper crockery; they are a good idea anyway, as they save washing-up. It is always a good plan to have a thermos filled with hot drink stowed within easy reach of the cockpit as well as a box of sweets and biscuits for the crew to nibble. If we look at the stores for a crew of eight who are taking part in a weekend race that starts on Saturday morning at 1000, it could look like this. We will assume that they will have already eaten breakfast prior to leaving the dock.

Saturday lunch

16 baps or hamburger-type buns with assorted fillings
8 Mars bars
8 apples
8 canned drinks
1 thermos of hot drink
    snack box filled with biscuits, sweets, etc.

Saturday supper

soup or pâté and biscuits
substantial main course pre-made and heated in the oven
potatoes and vegetables, pressure cooked or reheated in oven
pudding: trifle or apple pie for example
    cheese and biscuits
(It is a good idea if the person in charge of preparing supper also fills one or two thermos flasks for the night watches.)

Sunday breakfast

1 packet of bacon
8 eggs
    hash or French toast (pre-made)
2 loaves of bread
1lb butter
1 jar of marmalade
2 litres milk
1 packet of cereal
1 packet of sugar

Sunday lunch

16 chicken drumsticks (pre-cooked)
8 beef and onion loaf
    fruit cake, brownies, cheese, fruit and chocolate
8 cans of drink
Sundry items should include 10 gallons of water, tea-bags, coffee, Bovril and extra snacks such as dried fruit and nuts.

THE LONGER PASSAGE

A five-day or week's race is not difficult to cater for as there are enough varieties of boil-in-the-bag type meals available to have a different one every night. If the yacht has an insulated box, frozen main-course meals are no problem if you can get hold of a lump of dry ice. For the other meals I recommend dividing the day's rations into separate boxes or plastic crates, which are ideal.

Galley Routine

Although some owners prefer to do all the cooking and navigating themselves, there are those that ship someone whose only job is to cook. Then there are a few people who hope that the shapely blonde imported for the weekend can be coerced into cooking too. But more often than not, it is assumed that the skipper's wife will do everything from standing watch, navigating, foredeck hand, as well as being the head chef and bottle-washer. Of course, some people like it that way, in which case, so long as they are happy, all is well. We find that a little routine for galley assistance, where the crew share the tasks, is much appreciated. For example, the watch on deck should always do the washing-up and spud peeling. The cook might well appreciate having one day off a week on a long cruise, with the rest of the crew taking it in turns to be cook for the day; if no particular person is the overall cook, then work on a rota so that everyone cooks in turn. This routine usually ends up being fearfully competitive as each person out-cooks the others.

Organize the day's stores so that they can easily be retrieved from the bilges after breakfast so that sleeping bodies do not have to be disturbed unnecessarily later in the day. Someone, and it is usually the head cook, should keep the stores list up to date as well as turning over the fruit and vegetables, discarding anything that has gone rotten.

When sailing two-handed, one of us is in charge of breakfast, the other dinner, with self-service midday, a system that works well for us. Our two-handed watch-keeping system allows each of us a four-hour stretch off watch during the day, an hour together for lunch and a two-hour 'happy' hour in the evening when the navigational subcommittee meets to discuss serious topics, such as where we are, and then dinner *à deux*. We keep short watches during the night; two hours on if the weather is foul, three if all is peaceful.

A well-organized boat has a watch-keeping system which allows for a rotation of duties including everything from cleaning the heads to scrubbing the decks. It was interesting to learn that the English mariners who went aboard Spanish ships during the Armada were horrified by the appalling stench and squalor they encountered, even when their own shipboard habits were none too good. Sir William Monson wrote in his essay, 'The Ill-management of the Spanish Ships': 'Their ships are kept foul and beastly like hog-sties and sheep-cots in comparison with ours. And no marvel,' he continues, 'for no one on board was in charge of swabbing down the decks, and there was no galley to feed the entire company. Every man is his own cook, and he that is not able to dress his meat may fast.'

Planning the stores list

It is the calculation of the amount of food required for the six-week passage that can be quite a headache. When thinking about catering, bear in mind that food is fuel and for the crew to perform at maximum efficiency the carbohydrate and protein intake should be as high as possible. Carbohydrates such as bread, potatoes, cereals, dried fruit, chocolate and pulses are all converted by the body into instant energy, while milk, meat, fish, eggs, nuts and cheese are all high in protein and fats which are vital for stamina. The ideal diet is one that is nutritious, easy to digest and provides sufficient variety.

Working out the amount that a crew will consume over a given period of time is complicated enough; it is made more difficult by the unpredictability of the weather and other events, which means that if you have worked out your stores list on the basis of three meals a day, you could end up with a surplus since there are plenty of days when circumstances dictate that you eat less; equally there could be a deficiency if something goes badly wrong. Robin Knox-Johnston had the inspiration of shipping Clement Freud as cook on board for the first Cape Town-to-Rio Race. He recalls it was the finest eating he has ever experienced at sea. Clement used to get up at five each morning to bake the bread, and after fifteen days came to them and said, in his inimitable fashion, that they had a choice of steak, venison, gammon steak, or lamb cutlets (all of which they knew he would cook superbly). They asked why the choice and he told them that the dry ice had run out, so now was their last meat meal.

Water is the easiest equation to work out if you use the formula of allowing two pints a day per person. If your tank holds thirty gallons, this would mean that you have enough water for a crew of four for thirty days. This may sound Spartan but this refers only to drinking water; dishes, bodies and hair are washed in salt water. Ordinary shampoo lathers nicely in salt water; there is no need to buy expensive salt-water soap. Washing-up liquid works well, too, and can also be used as shampoo, but it is a bit harsh on hands and hair if used too frequently. I would rather wash my hair in salt water than not wash it at all and I find that a cup of fresh water for the final rinse is sufficient to remove most of the salt. Wet Ones and other kinds of wipes are refreshing and good for keeping yourself clean, especially when the weather is cold and rough. Rainwater can be caught in a bucket or some other receptacle fixed under the goose-neck fitting or the end of the boom, but don't use the first lot of water as it will be tainted by salt from the sails.

To calculate the amount of vegetables required to make salads depends on whether you are serving one or several kinds. Generally speaking, the more salads served, the less people will eat of any one salad. If you are serving only one kind, allow 1½ portions each. Conversely, if ten crew members are to choose from five different salads, allow a total of fifteen portions – i.e. three portions of each salad.

Vegetables
Carrot – 1lb (450g) grated, serves 4–5
Coleslaw – 1 medium hard cabbage serves at least 10
Green salad – 1 medium cos serves 6
(Lettuce) – 1 medium Webb or iceberg serves at least 8
1 medium Dutch serves 4–6
Potato salad – 1lb (450g) serves 4
Tomato salad – 1lb (450g) serves 4

Miscellaneous
Bread – A large sliced loaf generally has 18–20 slices. A crew of 4
  will eat a loaf a day if they have sandwiches for lunch
Butter – 1oz (30g) per head if bread is served with a meal and 1½oz
  (45g) if cheese is served as well. Soft spread margarine goes
  further

Cheese – After a meal: if only one kind, allow 3oz (85g) per head.
As a meal allow for 4oz (110g) per serving
Milk – 1 pint (600ml) = 18 cups of tea or coffee. Allow 2oz (60ml)
per head for cereal

Meat
Beef – Roast, stewed or steaks, allow 8oz (225g) per person. This
allows for trimming off fat and bone
Lamb – Roast 4½lbs (2kg) serves 6
Minced meat – 4oz (110g) per person for shepherd's pie or
hamburgers, lasagne, moussaka; 2oz (60g) per person for
spaghetti
Fish – Off the bone in fish pie 4oz (170g) per person
Prawns – 3oz (90g) per person as a generous starter

Planning the stores depends on the kind of cruise being contemplated.
First of all, will you be at sea for the whole duration, i.e., an Atlantic
crossing, or will it be a three-week cruise with a two-to-three-day
passage at either end and port-hopping in between? Second, what
sort of shopping facilities can you expect when you get there? Third,
what stores are not available where you are going? Finally, and probably most important of all, what items, if any, are cheaper bought
abroad? Chartering in countries like Turkey and Greece, for instance,
you may find basics such as instant coffee, cereals and the ubiquitous
baked beans and tomato ketchup are at least three times more
expensive.

Having taken that into account, it is pretty obvious that the majority
of items on the basic stores list are best bought at home, including
the household basics such as loo paper, kitchen towels etc: if you are
intending to head for the coast of France, then virtually all the contents
of the drinks locker can be bought more cheaply there, except for
whisky and gin. If you are setting off for the delightful cruising
grounds of the Baltic, don't forget that not only is alcohol prohibitively
expensive there, but so is everything else. The attraction of cruising
the wild coasts of Scotland and Ireland is the scenic beauty as well
as the solitary anchorages. Shopping is something you will do perhaps
once a week and then only for the staple items. If on your way up the
Irish coast, call in at Crosshaven where you will be sure of a fine

welcome from the Royal Cork Yacht Club, and while there, visit Mr Kidney the Butcher – his beef is excellent.

I find the easiest way of drawing up the stores list is to work on the principle of having two cooked meals a day, breakfast and dinner, with lunch consisting of soup and salad with cold meat, pâté or bread and cheese. More often than not the type of weather dictates what you feel like eating; your body soon tells you what it needs, such as salt in very hot weather, sugar in cold.

Buying ready-made meals from the chilled-food section in a supermarket is an extravagant method of catering, albeit convenient. The economical method is to pre-cook a number of dishes at home and then transport them to the boat in an insulated cold-box. If you don't have a deep-freeze on board, as long as your cold-box is well insulated, pre-frozen food will last for a couple of days. If you can buy a block of dry ice, frozen food will last for at least a week. Dry ice is preferable, as it evaporates instead of melting, but do take care when handling and use gloves, otherwise it will burn your hands quite badly. It can be difficult to know where to find dry ice, so ask your local fishmonger – usually a good source of information. If you are using a block of ordinary ice, which lasts longer than a bag of cubes, make sure that your ice-box has a drain hole which is protected with a grill, so that it does not get blocked with soggy paper. You can make your own blocks of ice at home. To retain the insulation, when you remove a box of food replace it with newspaper, or a block of polystyrene cut to size. Also, avoid opening the cold-box or fridge more often than necessary.

If we took a crew of six who were planning a three-week cruise from the south coast of England to south Brittany, how much of what should they take with them? First of all the passage plan. Let us assume that they have taken their boat down to the West Country in preparation for the Channel crossing and intend to leave from somewhere like Plymouth and go direct in one leg out to La Rochelle. From there they work their way back up the coast and think that the last port of call might be Benodet or even Camaret. From there they plan to sail home in one leg. Plymouth to La Rochelle is 250 miles (approx.) and assuming that they will average 5.5 knots overall, it is a trip of about three days, assuming they are lucky with the weather; I should allow for four or even five if it looks as though it will be dead to windward all the way. While they are port-hopping they will either eat ashore or buy fresh and cook on board. The last leg of the journey back is about 150 miles, which in theory they should be able to do in twenty-seven hours, but again I should round the figure up to two days to allow for contingencies. I am also assuming that this crew plan to eat out quite frequently and will do a fair amount of shopping for fresh items from the market – fish, pâtés, fruit, vegetables, cheese, etc. – when they eat on board.

Here is a list of stores and suggestions for breakfast and lunch menus for the passage out and back. This is in no way mandatory as everyone has particular preferences and tastes, but it should give a fair idea of how to plan your own stores list.

Basic Stores

Tins

Anchovy fillets	2–3 tins
Baked beans	4 tins, more if preferred
Bovril	Or Marmite
Cereal	1 or more large packets depending on crew's appetite; it can be expensive to buy abroad
Chicken pie	6 individual oven-bake pies
Chilli-con-carne	3 tins
Chocolate	2 large bars for night watches
Clams	2 tins; brilliant with spaghetti
Cocoa	1 tin for hot drinks
Coffee	2 large jars of instant or 4 dozen sachets
Corned beef	3 tins
Cup-of-Soup	6 boxes (4 in each box)
Curry powder	Small tin
Dressings	1 ready-made French, 1 small jar of mayonnaise; buy real olive oil and mayonnaise when there
Flour	1lb (450g) or 1 tin of cornflour for sauces
Herbs	Mixed
Jam	Honey, marmalade or favourite spread
Meat, mince	3 tins
Milk	24 pints of longlife (cannot get it in France)
Oxo cubes	1–2 packets for hot drinks
Pasta	2lb (450g) = 2 pasta meals
Peas	2–3 packets dried

Rice   2lb (450g) = 2 rice meals
Sardines   6 tins: sardines are highly nutritious and a friend
                    of mine swears that, apart from whisky, you
                    need not bother with any other stores, but I'm
                    not so sure
Sauces   2–3 different types for spaghetti, etc.
Spices   Assorted; empty 35mm film containers are ideal
                    for small amounts
Steak and kidney   6 tinned pies to bake in the oven
Stock cubes   1–2 packets
Sugar   ½–1lb (depending how many of the crew take
                    it in tea and coffee)
Sweets   Boiled sweets for night watches
Tea   1 box of 60 bags
Tomato ketchup   Can be obtained almost anywhere
Tomato paste   1 tube concentrated paste
Tomatoes   6 tins; good in most dishes
Tuna   2–3 12oz tins (the French brands of tinned tuna
                    and other fish are more varied than those
                    bought in the UK so I usually stock up in France
                    for the rest of the year)

Fresh
Including pre-made meals stored in the ice-box for the trip out
Apples   2–4lb (1–2kg)
Bacon   6 vacuum packs; lasts well, and bacon is
                    expensive in France
Bread   3 large sliced loaves for outward leg; 2
                    pumpernickel loaves for emergencies
Butter   6lb (3kg) or 3lb (1.5kg) butter, 3lb (1.5kg)
                    margarine
Cabbage   1 small hard Dutch
Carrots   1lb (450g)
Celery   1 head
Cucumber   1
French toast   1–2 rounds per head, freezes well (pre-prepare)
Cheese   1 tub of Parmesan, 2lb Cheddar; the variety of
                    local cheeses is one of the delights of France

Eggs	2 doz for the outward passage; buy more on arrival
Grapefruit	3 or more
Kippers	Provided you don't mind the smell
Lettuce	1 cos, 2 iceberg
Main-course meals	3 pre-cooked; enough tins if necessary
Oranges	2lb 3oz (1kg)
Pâté	Fresh and 2–3 tins
Peppers	1 red, 1 green
Potatoes	5lb (2½kg); keep well
Pizza	3 large; will keep for 2–3 days if kept cool
Quiche	3 large; will keep for 2–3 days if kept cool
Tomatoes	2lb (1kg)

Non-consumable items
Clothes pegs
Drying-up cloths
Dustbin liners for non-biodegradable rubbish while at sea and all rubbish in port
General purpose cleaning fluid for galley and heads
Kitchen paper   3 rolls
Liquid detergent for washing clothes
Loo paper   12 rolls
Shampoo and soap
Washing-up liquid   1 large

Suggestions for:

Breakfast	*Lunch*
Baked beans	Tuna mayonnaise
Cereal	Coleslaw
Coffee, tea, sugar	Packet or home-made soup
Eggs, various	Pâté
Grapefruit	Toasted sandwiches with various fillings
Hash 'n' eggs	Oxo cubes, Bovril 'n' sherry
French toast	Chicken salad
Kippers	Salad Niçoise
Toast	Salad of various types
	Quiche, pizza

The drinks locker

When restocking the drinks locker, no doubt you will have taken into account that some spirits like whisky and gin will be more expensive abroad, but other spirits such as brandy and rum will be cheaper if bought from the local supermarket. Although beer and wine are cheaper on the Continent, I always take at least one box of wine to drink on the way, or in case we have an unscheduled stop where getting ashore to the bar may be difficult. I also recommend cramming the bilges with as many mixers and sodas (this includes beer) as possible. Apart from any other consideration, they are extremely heavy to have to hump back from the local shop, which could be miles away from your anchorage.

THE ATLANTIC PASSAGE

There are at least four well-known routes across the Atlantic. The first is to leave Plymouth and turn right for Newport, taking the great-circle route; second, the rhumb line; third via the Azores and Bermuda to New York or Newport. If heading for the lotus-eating areas of the West Indies, then you will probably take the advice of the old ship-masters and 'Go south till the butter melts, then turn west'. Having made your westing along latitude 17 or 18 N from a point SW of the Canaries, head NNW when about two days out from Antigua. It is a lot farther, and positively cries out for a stopover in English Harbour and Bermuda. This fourth route is extremely popular, as the weather is less inclement and a great deal warmer; it is sometimes known as the milk run.

If you take either of the northern routes, you can expect it to be cold and have several gales in the first half, fog and even ice in the second. But Cape Cod, New England and Maine are wonderful cruising grounds even if the fog can make navigation quite tricky. If you are in search of beautiful and unspoilt anchorages, whales and fabulous wildlife, as well as seafood specialities such as Cape Cod lobsters, clams and scallops, it is well worth the effort of getting there via the great-circle or rhumb-line route from England. (Most sensible people choose to cruise New England on their way home from the Atlantic circuit via the West Indies and Bermuda.)

The stores you take with you if you take the northern route are more likely to be substantial and warming: porridge, for example, is good for the morale when thrashing into grey-green breaking seas, whereas on the southern route, where the ambient temperature is warmer and the sun shines out of an azure sky, fresh melon is more appropriate for breakfast.

A crew of six planning a three-week passage across the Atlantic might stock up with the following fresh food. Without the resources of a fridge and only limited space in an ice-box, a pressure cooker comes into its own. The first night's dinner is cooked in the pressure cooker and tins of this and that added as and when required. You do not need a galley fitted out to the standards of the *QE2* to produce exceptional meals, and, with a little practice and determination, nor do you need a flat calm, although it does make life a little easier.

Robin Knox-Johnston and his loyal crew, Billy King-Harman, were hove-to in a hurricane off Santo Domingo. As it was also Christmas Day, Robin thought that they needed a little treat, so he made a bully-beef curry, two varieties, one hot and one medium. (All this was cooked on a two-burner gas cooker and the saucepans had to be held on the rings.) Not to be outdone, Billy then produced a peach flambé for pudding, which was delicious and much appreciated.

The following suggestions deal mainly with fresh stores rather than covering the whole of the list in detail. By using the basic stores list and some of the suggestions for the holiday cruise as a guide, it should be fairly simple to work out the full stores list for a long passage.

Fruit and Vegetables

Apples	2 boxes
Avocados	24
Bananas	5kg
Cabbage	6 large hard
Carrots	2kg
Garlic	6 bulbs, or more
Grapefruit	2 sacks (approx 25 per sack)
Lemons	30
Melons	3
Onions	2 x 10kg
Oranges	3 sacks (approx 20 per sack)
Pineapples	3
Potatoes	3 x 15kg
Tomatoes	2 boxes (1 green, 1 semi-ripe)

Bread

Half cooked	24 loaves; one will serve two, nice as a a treat
Pumpernickel	6 loaves – lasts almost indefinitely
Ryebread	3 loaves – lasts the same as wholemeal, but nice as a change
Wholemeal sliced	12 loaves – will last about ten days before going mouldy

Cheese

Camembert	2 boxes
Cheddar	1 whole truckle
Emmental	
Gouda	1 whole
Parmesan	2 x 8oz tubs
Port Salut	2
Stilton	1 small

Meat

Bacon	6 packets (1 packet per breakfast)
Beef	12 steaks, frozen
Beef, salted	1 joint
Ham	1 whole
Lamb	2 legs, 1 frozen, 1 fresh
Salami	2–3 assorted
Tinned	Various assorted tins including a selection of pâtés

Fish

Tuna, sardines, salmon, prawns, etc, all tinned

Kippers	12 pairs

Miscellaneous

Butter	8.8lb (4kg)
Cereal	4.6lb (2kg) assorted
Eggs	4 doz
Milk	24 litres longlife
Milk	1 tin dried

Alcohol

Most owners have at least one drink during the happy hour, and wine with the evening meal.

Brandy	1 bottle
Gin	3 bottles
Rum	3 bottles
Vodka	3 bottles
Whisky	3 bottles
Wine, red	12 bottles
Wine, white	12 bottles
Beer	10 doz

Non-Alcoholic Drinks

Lime juice	3 bottles
Orange juice	6 litres
Sodas	10 doz assorted canned drinks
Squash, lemon and orange	4 litres
Tomato juice	6 litres

A word of warning: it is vitally important that you have absolute confidence in the person you delegate to go off on the final shopping spree prior to departure for a longish sail or you may end up with a rather restricted diet. There was once a crew member who was sent off to purchase all the provisions for a trip from Gibraltar to Malta. She must have found a major distraction ashore, or perhaps she was just tired and emotional, because two days out the crew discovered that all they had left on board in the way of food was a mountain of cornflakes and curry powder.

CHAPTER FIVE

Alcoholic Stores –
Dry Ship or Not?

If all be true that I do think,
There are five reasons we should drink;
Good wine – a friend – or being dry –
Or lest we should be by and by –
Or any other reason why.
Dean Aldrich, *Reasons for Drinking*

There are some who frown at the thought of carrying any alcohol on board a yacht in racing trim; there are others who go to the opposite extreme. Unless you find yourself skipper of a crew of devout Muslims, a certain amount of booze is essential to the general happiness of the crew – racing or cruising. There are, however, some people who never know when to stop. I have heard stories, no doubt apocryphal, regarding skippers who spend most of the day guzzling the hard stuff down below until they are completely blotto and then emerge on deck only to wrench the wheel out of the helmsman's grasp, gybe the ship all-standing, and then stagger back below muttering; 'Now sort that out you b . . .' Moderation is the name of the game, and enlightened owners allow wine with the evening meal. Most racing men save the hard stuff until crossing the finishing line, when everyone gets plastered long before reaching the dock.

On the other hand, there may be some who have been listening to members of the medical profession and other health-conscious voices of warning, and now hesitate as they pour that third tumblerful of whisky before relieving the watch. As an extreme example, taken from the United States Naval Archives, the following account of the voyage of the USS *Constitution* in the eighteenth century hardly makes that ship's crew look like fully paid up members of the Temperance League.

The USS *Constitution* set sail from Boston on 23 August 1779 with

475 officers and men, on a mission to harry and destroy English shipping. She was victualled with 48,600 gallons of fresh water, ample ship's biscuit and beef, 7,400 cannon shot, 11,600lb of black powder, and 7,940 gallons of rum. She made Jamaica on 6 October and took on board 862lb flour and 6,830 gallons of rum. She then headed for the Azores, arriving on 12 November, and was provisioned with 550lb of beef and 6,430 gallons of Portuguese wine. On 18 November she set sail for England and, in the ensuing days, defeated five British men-of-war, and captured and scuttled twelve English merchantmen, salvaging only their rum. By 27 January her powder and shot were exhausted. Unarmed, she made a raid up the Firth of Clyde and her landing party captured a whisky distillery, and transferred 4,000 gallons on board by dawn. She then headed home and arrived Boston harbour on 20 February 1780, six months after raising anchor, with no cannon shot, no powder, no food, no rum, no whisky, but with 48,600 gallons of stagnant water. This meant that each man had consumed nearly two pints of spirits per day plus about half a pint of wine. No wonder this particular ship was called the *Constitution*.

Sailing is thirsty work. The salt-laden atmosphere is one factor; the other is the amount of fluid lost through evaporation, especially if sailing in hot climates. One August we took the family on a flotilla cruise in Turkey. It was a year when the Mediterranean had a heat wave for several weeks and there were reports in the English papers of people dying of sunstroke. Our flotilla leader advised us to eat a teaspoon of salt every day and to drink as much water as possible. It was exceptionally hot. The wind, instead of having a cooling effect, was more like having a hot hair-drier blowing in your face all night and, despite following his advice, most of us were knocked out by the heat for a couple of days, though the teaspoon of salt certainly helped.

DUTY FREE

If setting off across the Atlantic for the Caribbean with a crew of six, you may think it is worth all the paperwork and trouble to arrange for bonded stores, which have to be sealed in lockers prior to departure. On the other hand, it is probably far easier simply to call in at a port in France and take on board wines and spirits from any supermarket. The only significant saving to be made by buying duty free in this country is in buying spirits and tobacco.

Beer – This covers all the enormous range of fermented hop and barley products ranging from real beer, bitter, mild, lager, stout and Guinness. Even racing skippers in the States who run 'dry' ships allow unlimited beer, as they classify it as 'soda'.

Champagne – When Desmond and I competed in our first-ever ocean race, the 1979 Round Britain Race, his ever-generous partners gave us a case of half-bottles of champagne. It was much appreciated and, as we squeaked round Portland Bill on the inshore passage, we popped the last cork, which reached the shore. Johnnie Coote advises that a few bottles should always be smuggled on board for That Special Occasion, like thinking you have won the Fastnet. He usually celebrates his birthday on the Fastnet. Once he worked out that they would be safely round the Bishop and heading for home that evening, so he secreted a case on board, having first issued embossed formal invitations to an 'At Home' in Lat. and Long. at the point they should have been at 7knots speed overall. In fact, they crossed the finish at 0900 that morning, so the whole of Plymouth drank his champagne.

Gin – Apart from drinking with the usual mixers of tonic, Martini, orange juice or bitters, it is good for marinating and preserving an excess of freshly caught fish (see recipes).

Non-alcoholic beer – I can't see the point of this unless you are on a fiendishly strict diet.

Rum – 'Grog' was the invention of Admiral Edward Vernon when in command of the West Indies fleet in 1740. The daily allowance of half a pint of rum per man was diluted with a quart of water and issued twice a day, in order, said Vernon, to drive 'that Dragon Drunkenness, out of the Fleet'. Surgeons and admirals continued to complain about the evil effects of the ration, so generous that half the ship's company might be inebriated in the afternoon watch. Life on board in those days was hard, and grog was sacrosanct; indeed, it alone made the conditions tolerable. I was introduced to the delights of Pusser's Navy Rum by an ex-serviceman as an early-morning hot toddy. There is no doubt that a liberal measure added to orange juice and hot water will effectively reduce the wind force by a few knots. If you need to reassure your conscience, if you have been on watch from 0400–0800 on a cold, wet and windy morning and your body clock is telling you that it is at least 1200, it is quite permissible to have a drink. Apart from Pusser's, other good dark rum varieties are St James which can be found in most French ports and, in Bermuda, Goslings. Mount Gay is a lighter Barbados rum and cheap in the USA. Dark rum can be mixed with anything to make a good drink. Try it with real ginger beer – a 'Dark 'n' Stormy' – or Rose's Lime Juice.

Vodka – Delicious, also important equipment for repairing compasses. Once while racing we developed an enormous bubble in our main compass so we decided to hold a compass-adjusting party, and proceeded to make our own repairs by injecting vodka. It was quite successful, but by the end of the season the fluid appeared cloudy so we sent the compass off to Sestrel More. When they returned it there was a stiff bill enclosed for 'removing alien fluid'.

Whisky – (A certain lady was intrigued by the nightly activities of the owner she was sailing with as crew. By the light of the moon she could just see into the after cabin and noticed the owner's hand as he poured himself a drink. She remembers thinking, what a good man, all he drinks is Lucozade. Several nights later the moonlit hand was definitely trembling. When she turned in, she opened the booze locker under her bunk to discover that there were no longer fifty bottles of whisky but twenty-nine.) I use Bell's or Johnnie Walker for the evening 'tot'. It is also good in whisky butter to go with mince pies or Christmas pudding. Malt whisky is ideal for that special occasion when you beat a previous best day's run, or worse.

Wine – The advent of boxed wine is the best invention since sliced bread. The empty bags can be inflated and used as pillows or balloons to keep small and not so small children amused. Buy your wine from French supermarkets. Beer is also very good value in France. Beware of cheap Spanish red wine, not nicknamed 'The Red Infuriator' for nothing. I am advised that when you buy Rioja remember that any bottle over ten years old is bound to be good.

Port – Much appreciated by all and sundry when sailing during the winter in the Solent. Try mixing it half and half with rum or brandy. (This is apparently the favourite tipple of the South Australians, who supplied all the foreign yachts in the Hobart Race one year with bottles of rum and port ready mixed, although not many of them had a chance to sample it: it was a particularly stormy race and most of the bottles were smashed *en route*.)

Mixers – In the USA, carbonated drinks are lumped together as 'sodas'. This covers everything from Coke (diet or plain), Pepsi, Orangina, tonic, Fanta, psschtt, etc. Soda water is referred to as Club Soda in the States.

Fruit drinks – Long-life, fresh-fruit drinks are always welcome and come in a wide variety. The individual packs with a straw are more expensive but as there is no waste from spillage or going off, they are to my way of thinking well worth the extra expense, especially when sailing short-handed or with children.

Squash – Orange, lemon, barley water, and lime juice in particular, which is delicious with almost anything (Gimlets, for example), or just with ice and bottled mineral water.

Tomato juice – For 'Bloody' or 'Virgin Marys'. Also good as a basis for Gazpacho soup.

Water – Any of the fizzy bottled waters like Perrier, Sparkling Malvern or any other brand name are good on their own or mixed with fruit juice, squash or wine.

Recipes

RUM

It is said that whisky makes a girl stop arguing, beer soothes her, gin disarms her, rum cajoles.

21 club cocktail (Bermuda)
1 measure of rum
1 measure of Cointreau
1 measure of freshly squeezed orange juice
Shake with crushed ice and serve

Port in a storm
½ glass port
½ glass rum

Dark 'n' stormies
1 measure of rum
real ginger beer

The hot toddy
1 measure of rum
orange or lemon squash diluted with hot water
Add a pat of butter and sugar

Rum sour
1 measure of rum
juice of ½ lemon
½ tsp sugar
dash of Angostura bitters
ice and soda water

VODKA
Screwdriver
1 measure of vodka
fresh orange juice
ice

Bullshots
(or **Ox-on-the-rocks**)
vodka
beef consommé
oregano
lime juice
tabasco sauce

Gorilla fodder – After the race is over . . .
measure of 100% proof vodka
cold beer
dash of tabasco sauce

Planter's Punch
large measure of rum
juice of ½ lemon *or*
1 whole lime
1 tsp sugar
soda

Bloody Mary
1 measure of vodka
tomato juice
juice of ½ lemon
Worcestershire Sauce and celery
salt

GIN
In Hogarth's heyday, it was estimated that one house in four in London was a gin shop. More than likely there was a creaking sign outside which declared, 'Here a man may get drunk for one penny and dead drunk for twopence.'

Tom Collins
1 measure of gin
juice of 1 lemon
1 tsp sugar
ice
Top up with fizzy water

Gin Stinger
1½ measures of gin
¾ measure of white crème de
menthe
lemon peel
plenty of ice

Gimlet
1½oz gin
juice of ½ lime
¼ tsp maraschino liqueur
dash of bitters
ice
Daiquiri
1½oz light rum – Mount Gay
juice of ½ large lime
1 tsp sugar

The Martini
Advice to WRNS sent to USA during the Second World War:

> Beware the American Martini,
> Never take two at the most.
> Three and you're under the table;
> Four and you're under your host.

3 measures of gin
½ measure of dry vermouth
plenty of ice
1 green olive or twist of lemon
Shake or stir; it makes no difference, regardless of James Bond's prejudices.

CHAPTER SIX

Keeping Warm and Dry

Not so long ago, some people considered spray hoods slightly sissy; no doubt they also held the opinion that being cold and wet on watch, taking the wind and weather on the chin, was an essential part of real yachting. They are most likely the same people who despised any modern gadget, depth sounders, for example. You will hear them say, 'Nice idea, but of course it'll never catch on – what's wrong with the good old lead line?' Luddites never proved anything, except that progress may be resisted but never halted. People have gradually come round to the idea that there is no need to sit totally unprotected in the cockpit and that spray hoods and 'dog-houses' can improve the overall appearance of yachts. But there is still one design feature that is frequently overlooked, and that is where to put wet oilskins, for, despite spray hoods and self-steering gear, just occasionally you still have to go on deck and get wet in the process.

Lockers for hanging clothes are a problem on small yachts. Sometimes the only space available for wet oilskins to drip-dry is situated well forward, opposite the heads. This is fine in theory but in practice it leaves much to be desired, as the crew are bound to tramp through the saloon and saturate everything *en route*. What is really needed is somewhere where the crew coming off watch can leave their wet jackets and trousers to drip so that the minimum amount of water gets into the saloon area. This is where a good spray hood partially solves the problem, as it gives enough protection to enable you to remove your jacket, at least. If there is no space around the galley or navigatorium for a permanent wet locker, then a couple of stout hooks either side of the companion-way steps will have to suffice. This still leaves the problem of stopping the water brought below from getting all through the boat. A batten on the cabin sole between the saloon and the chart area may deflect the worst of the water brought below.

The best way of protecting your smarter shore-going clothes if they have to live cheek-by-jowl with wet oilskins is to invest in a PVC hanging bag, that holds a dinner jacket and a couple of suits. A cheaper way round the same problem is either to use a dry cleaner who offers a valet service, which means that your suit is returned on a decent hanger inside a nice thick plastic bag, or make friends with your local dry cleaner who provides this service, and persuade him to let you have a couple of the bags anyway.

Sailing in European waters seems to be a constant war of attrition against the elements, therefore it is hardly surprising that many of the best oilskins and thermal clothes have been designed and made by British manufacturers. There is a real danger of becoming hypothermic through inadequate clothing, especially in the early part of the year when the air is denser and colder than in the autumn. It is the duty of the skipper to ensure that new or novice crew are properly equipped for the type of passage to be undertaken. The classic example of inadequate clothing is the man who has only jeans, a couple of shirts and a jersey to wear under his oilskins, which provide little or no insulation.

The biggest problems in keeping warm are evaporation and insulation. Conversely, the same is true of keeping cool. Any undergarment must be able to draw perspiration away from the skin and into the outer garments by a capillary action, if the body is to remain warm and dry. Musto and Hyde make suits of polypropylene which has been successfully tested in the Whitbread Round the World Race. The intermediate layer, designed for insulation, has an outer covering of nylon which provides some protection against wear and can be worn as external clothing if the weather permits. The latest research shows that Thinsulate has twice the thermal properties of polyester, fibrefill, down or pile without any increase in bulk or weight. Some of these suits are designed in one piece, but they are not very practical when nature calls, unless there is a flap in the back as well as the front.

BEDDING

Many years ago I remember being so cold that I resorted to lining my bunk with old newspapers, which, as anyone who sleeps rough will tell you, provide excellent insulation. Today, I sleep in a bean bag which is made by the same people who make Dognests. Even when damp, it still feels warm. Polycotton inner bags save having to wash sleeping bags more often than necessary, pillowcases as well. The Dognest company also make quilted scarves and waistcoats which are comfortable to wear and very warm. Duvets are becoming popular to replace sleeping bags, but there is always the problem of stowing them away during the day. They are best confined to the owner's cabin.

CLOTHING

Boots

The standard cloth-lined rubber boots are fine for most sailing situations, and will keep your feet warm provided they are big enough to allow for a good thermal sock and boot lining. Equinox make excellent linings which are warm and fast drying. For really cold conditions, like the South Atlantic, insulated soles can be bought to go inside the boots.

Gloves

Leather fingerless gloves are perfectly adequate for most of the time but they do not keep the hands warm or dry. A pair of large mittens over the top will certainly keep your hands warm; the problem is keeping the water out. The lifeboat crews and fishermen use cotton-based industrial gloves which have been dipped in PVC, but ordinary heavyweight rubber gloves worn over Thinsulate glove linings are almost as good. Ski-mitts are warm and can be clipped to your jacket cuff so that they are not lost if you need to take them off in a hurry. To prevent your hands chapping and becoming generally rough and sore, buy pure saturated lanolin from a chemist; it is very sticky, but it protects your hands and keeps them in good condition. Alternatively, buy unwashed wool and knit your own mittens, hats, socks and jerseys.

Hats

It is said that 25 per cent of body heat is lost through the head, so a Balaclava or woolly hat is essential. In really cold weather I wear a silk skiing Balaclava under a woolly hat, which is nicely cosy and has the added bonus of being less irritating to the skin. The old offshore fisherman's hat (Grand Banks sou'westers in the States), with a long overhanging brim, is the best way of stopping water penetrating down the back of your neck.

Foul Weather Gear

For day racing or sailing during the summer months, cheap lightweight oilskins are quite sufficient. For offshore sailing oilskins need to be sophisticated and should have a harness that is integral with the jacket. Even when day sailing, the importance of keeping a harness and line aboard your boat for each crew member cannot be exaggerated. Everyone must know where they are kept. Harness lines, which you hook on to your jacket in rough weather, are best kept hooked on to the attachment point in the cockpit with another hanging down inside the cabin, so, as a man comes up on deck, the line is already in place; all he has to do is clip himself on. Coming up on deck when half asleep is probably the time when you are most at risk and could easily be thrown overboard in severe weather, as the yacht falls off the top of a big wave. It is worth bearing in mind that, if your boat has patches of Treadmaster or non-slip deck paint, your oilskins will wear out on the seat and knees much sooner than if the decks are teak or moulded fibreglass. The manufacturers of your oilskins will put extra patches on if you ask them. Some yachts are much wetter on the foredeck than others, in which case a 'drysuit' top is useful to have if you are going to do a lot of changing sails. The best solution, and one which has grown enormously in popularity in the last five years, is to have a furling headsail.

Drying-out Clothes

If there is one thing as miserable as putting on a wet swimming costume, it's pulling on wet socks. Apart from praying for a fine day, the only alternative is to use the heat generated by the engine for drying out socks, hats and gloves. A simple way of doing this is to fix a basket on the inside of the engine cover, first making sure that there is enough space and that it will not get in the way of the fly wheel.

One year, instead of taking the usual umpteen pairs of knickers I tried using paper ones. They were not a success: within an hour or two they disintegrated, leaving me with three uncomfortable pieces of elastic. It may sound extravagant, but when I know that washing and drying 'smalls' is going to be difficult, I take my oldest pairs of cotton

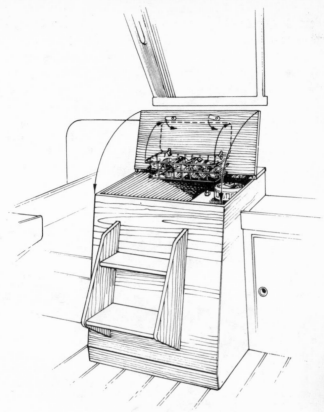

13. Drying socks, gloves and hats

knickers which I don't mind jettisoning. Cotton is by far the most comfortable texture to wear next to the skin.

Keeping Cool

It is as rare to see a sun awning or a wind-scoop rigged on a yacht riding at anchor in this country as it is to see the lesser spotted bikini bird who is a shy creature at sea during our summer season. Even when those ashore are sizzling in suntan oil, the breeze at sea has a definite cooling effect on the temperature, so it is easy to ignore the warning signals of lobster-coloured flesh.

There is a bewildering range of tanning products on the market, many more now than a few years ago. Reported cases of skin cancers, once rare in this country and America, have increased in the last few years, so doctors warn us against the dangers of over-exposure to the sun. Most, if not all, brands of sun cream have a high screening factor and some a total sun block. The higher the number, the greater the protection, and the longer you can stay in the sun. Thus factor 5 in a range from 1–10 is formulated to provide normal protection for the first exposure to the sun by easy tanners, dark-skinned types like Latin Americans, for example, or people already with a tan. Factor 10 is for fair-skinned people, who always go red before developing a tan, and people with delicate skins, children in particular.

Sailors and skiers are equally at risk from reflection off the sea and snow. Sensitive skins, including children's, need initially a product with a high screening factor even when the weather is hazy. Water-resistant sunscreens are especially good as they need to be re-applied less often. The areas most at risk are shoulders, tops of thighs, backs of knees, ears, noses and bald pates. Peaked caps and solar topis are useful; a handkerchief draped down the back of the neck will protect a vulnerable part that is apt to turn turkey-cock red. (The English were called rednecks in various parts of the Empire because of this very problem.) Especially in the Mediterranean be sure to take long-sleeved cotton shirts with collars. Before you cover yourself in thick sticky oil and stretch out on a scrubbed teak deck, be warned that some suntan oils contain an ingredient which stains fabric and teak decks.

Eyes are particularly vulnerable to glare at sea, so a good quality pair of sun-glasses with Polarized lenses are more than just a fashion accessory. Cheap sun-glasses with poor quality lenses can do more harm than good if worn for long periods in bright sunny weather; it is worth paying a little more for better protection. If in any doubt, ask an optician.

Unless you have cruised in hot climates it is difficult to appreciate the need for a sun awning or wind-scoop. If you are planning to sail to the Mediterranean or West Indies, both items should be high on the list of priorities. Geoff Pack in his book, *Ocean Cruising Countdown*, describes how to make a full-size awning that stretches from the cockpit to the mast, thus keeping the accommodation cool and venti-lated, as well as a small awning covering the cockpit that can be rigged when sailing in moderate weather to provide essential shade during the hottest hours of the day.

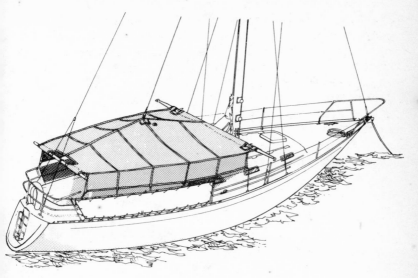

14. Full-size awning

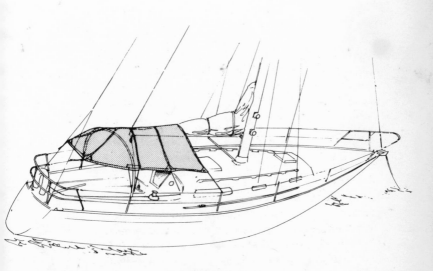

15. Short awning

CHAPTER SEVEN

Animals and Other Friends

ANIMALS

When our children were young we spent a number of years sailing in company with friends and their children of similar ages. We also had dogs in common. Ours was a small rough-coated terrier of rather dubious pedigree. I must admit that she never really took to sailing although she put up with it stoically, except when she was rowed ashore in a wet and wobbling rubber dinghy for her evening walk. Our friend's dog was a large and boisterous retriever who added to the general mayhem by leaping on board after a swim and shaking mud and water everywhere and then settling down to have a good chew on whatever piece of rope was at hand. Annabel tried every conceivable trick to get him to use the stanchions to pee against, even to the lengths of taking them home in the winter and planting them in the garden in the hopes that this would encourage him to use them the next summer; he never even gave them as much as a sniff.

Cats, on the other hand, seem to take to life aboard with great aplomb and have sailed long distances with their families. This is the place to reiterate the warning that no livestock of any kind may be imported into this country without the proper documentation and arrangements for quarantine. Even having your pet on board and not letting it ashore if you cross the Channel is illegal and will result in a heavy fine and probable destruction of the animal.

CHILDREN

Our children had their first taste of salt spray as they gazed at the world from a carry-cot. Holidays afloat were something, so they tell me now, up with which they put. Children (at least ours did) seem to take up twice the space of adults on small boats. It is not so much their size as the size of their accompanying families of teddies, Snoopy, and Sindy dolls.

The problem is, where do you stow them all: their toys, not the children. The shelves behind the saloon seats and in the fo'c'sle either side of the berths were favourite places for converting into bunks, beds and nesting places for teddy and friends, which was fine so long as you remembered to give them prior notice of impending changes, of course. Are we the only people to have gone aground in the Beaulieu River because Snoopy wasn't ready to tack when we were?

We always kept a large supply of paper, pencils and colouring pens at hand which occupied the youngsters for most of the time. While encouraging the educational value of paper and pencils, beware of their own built-in hazards. After all, who can blame any small child who has watched Mummy or Daddy draw lines and squiggles on that nice big sheet of paper for following suit. Our charts were under constant surveillance by the junior chart correctors, who loved to draw in nice big red buoys (or was it boys). One afternoon we suddenly noticed an ominous peace from below and saw two heads bent studiously over the chart table; they were joining up the soundings like a dot-to-dot picture, hoping to make a masterpiece.

We had extra-large lee-cloths fitted, which were a boon for really small children on passage as they were snug and safe. When they were asleep it didn't matter which tack we were on, unlike one family I know whose small child fell asleep on the main sheet in the cockpit and as they did not have the heart to wake him up, they continued on the same tack for another three hours until he woke of his own accord.

One year we took our two girls across the Atlantic from Newport to the Azores, when they were eight and ten. It was a reasonably successful trip for two reasons. First of all, we were in the Gulf Stream which mean that, apart from the water being the most glorious temperature and just right for chucking buckets over one another, the Stream is itself a mini-ecosystem so the girls spent hours collecting buckets of weed from which they separated a host of little creatures. Vanessa had buckets, cups and pots jammed in all sorts of corners of the boat full of mini lobsters, crabs and a host of other creatures, all of which she christened individually. At night, there were stifled curses as one of us would trip over a bucket in the dark. At breakfast the wrath of Vanessa had to be faced when we owned up to the fact that Solomon and his harem had been lost down the cockpit drains. Apart from various toys and games, the success of the trip depended on the amount of involvement the children had in the day-to-day management and running of the boat. That Emma, aged ten, was taking just as good sun-sights as either of her parents, and working them out using NP tables, not a calculator, gave her a lot of satisfaction and was an enormous credit to her.

Card games were a great success until Father lost his sense of humour when Vanessa consistently won at poker and demanded the sum of £5 – we had been playing for halfpenny stakes. The highlight of that crossing was the Royal Wedding. This provided a wonderful excuse for dressing up and making splendidly unsuitable hats for the occasion. We listened to the service on the radio and later on, having taken down the spinnaker, we held our own party complete with candles, crackers and dancing on the foredeck with music full blast.

Other successful games were Hangman and Battleships, especially when we were within VHF range of other friends and could play them over the radio. It is probably not very wise to play Battleships over the radio when you are anywhere near a shipping lane as you never know who may be listening on the ship-to-ship channel. 'Warship, warship . . . hit and sink . . .' could result in World War III.

Now our girls are teenagers they spend most of their time with their earphones clamped to their heads. I am all in favour of 'Walkmans'. No longer do we have sulks and arguments as each individual tunes in to whatever turns them on without annoying anyone else. Walkmans do however have their disadvantages. If someone who is wired for sound sits in the cockpit close to the main compass unbeknown to the navigator, all kinds of navigational errors are bound to occur. The other problem is trying to attract the attention of someone who is plugged in. You can do a war dance on the foredeck, or a strip-tease in the cockpit, but they continue sitting there with glazed expression, heads nodding, lips moving silently, unless, of course, you happen to mention food or drink.

Part of the planning of what to take must include provision for recreation (as some people like to call it, the leisure hours). Now that navigation has become so 'High Tech' and the chart table is surrounded by enough instruments to equip a jumbo jet, there is often little space left for stowing the most important ingredient to happy cruising: the library. When my husband Desmond, and Giles Chichester raced in the last two-handed transatlantic race they took with them three books: two novels and the Bible. They were dismasted at the end of the first week, about 1,000 miles out from Plymouth, during a particularly vicious gale. When it had blown itself out they rigged a jury rig and turned back. Sod's Law being what it is, the wind obligingly went into the east and the 1,000 miles back took them two and a half weeks. The novels had been soaked and turned to pulp and the Bible was well thumbed by the time they got back.

The library, music tapes as well as books, should be as eclectic a choice as possible to cater for all tastes. Background music gently playing as the sun sinks below the waves is just like the ending of many a Hollywood movie, and there are plenty of moments when the right piece of music is the perfect complement or a contrast to the mood. I find that when the weather is foul, the precision of the point and counterpoint of a Bach concerto is a perfect contrast to the chaotic waves. The last thing I want to listen to in those conditions is boisterous Wagner. *Chacun à son goût*, as they say. Paperbacks, penny dreadfuls as my mother calls them, are essential for swapping with other crews when on longer cruises or in foreign parts. Apart from the library, board games such as travel Scrabble, chess, backgammon and liar dice are all popular, especially with a young crew; do not forget to take enough packs of cards for serious sessions of racing demon and bridge when the weather is calm.

CHAPTER EIGHT

Coping with Bad Weather – Preparing for the Worst

> *When the cabin port-holes are dark and green*
> > *Because of the seas outside;*
> *When the ship goes* wop *(with a wiggle between)*
> *And the steward falls into the soup-tureen,*
> > *And the trunks begin to slide;*
> *When Nursey lies on the floor in a heap,*
> *And Mummy tells you to let her sleep,*
> *And you aren't waked or washed or dressed,*
> *Why, then you will know (if you haven't guessed)*
> *You're 'Fifty North and Forty West!'*
> Rudyard Kipling, *Just So Stories*

Malin, Hebrides . . . Blast! Yet again the skipper has overslept and missed the forecast. Sooner or later you are bound to run into foul weather or a short sharp blow that catches you out as you scurry for home. Obviously, on longer passages it is almost inevitable that you will have one or more gales, or if you are really unlucky, one of those storms that are preferable read about while sitting in the comfort of an armchair. Although there are plenty of jokes about that well-known pair of comedians, McCaskill and Fish, on the whole the Met. Office does a good job. Listen to VHF, as the coastal radio stations give out weather forecasts for their immediate areas. If on ocean passages, a single side band radio, or a transistor that can receive short wave, is useful to pick up the World Wide Weather Service. The Admiralty List of Radio Signals gives the relevant information. Before setting out you can use the new Marinecall telephone service: (0898) 500 450 will give you a marine forecast for five days ahead.

The safest place to be in a gale is well off shore, assuming your craft is well found and there are no major dramas such as knockdowns, dismasting or gear failure. Although it may well be uncomfortable, noisy, and at times frightening, there is not a lot you can do about it, but no gale lasts for ever. Shipboard life is usually run around the forecast as it tends to be one of the social events of the day. A lot of the accuracy depends on where you are sailing. For example, around the west coasts of Scotland and Ireland, you may as well rely on a bit of seaweed as on the shipping forecast, or, at Valencia, you could try calling up the lighthouse keeper (his call sign is the same as his donkey's). Apart from radio forecasts, a barometer is a reliable indicator of future weather; the difficulty is in judging the duration of a blow and the speed at which the weather systems are moving. Learning to read the weather from the sky is a fascinating pastime and something that comes with practice. Alan Watts's book of weather forecasting for yachtsmen should be in your ship's library.

It is rare that a gale comes without any warning, except in the Mediterranean. When you suspect that bad weather is on its way the skipper should ensure that the boat is prepared for the blow. That also includes seeing that the crew are fed before it strikes and that there is something brewed up in the pressure cooker for later on. No one, apart from a few Spartan souls, actually enjoys the process of juggling pots and pans in the height of a gale, but the quickest way to cheer up the crew is to have something hot for them when they come off watch.

When discussing bad weather, most people think that you are referring to winds of Force 8 or more, but this is not necessarily so as bad weather is relative; beating to windward in Force 5 to 6 in a small boat is every bit as uncomfortable as in stronger winds in a bigger yacht. The sort of food to prepare in advance is really a matter of common sense; it should be good, filling food that is simple to digest. The other vital consideration is the morale of the crew: if their smiles have turned upside-down, then is the moment to produce a little surprise to cheer everyone up, like hot bread, for example. A friend of mine took her nephew and niece for a day sail when the youngest, Ione, was only four years old. There was quite a lot of wind and they were well reefed down. Just as they reached the bottom of the river a gust caught them and *Quixote* heeled sharply. Leo, aged eight, was delighted, but Ione was not so pleased – 'I wish we were at home,' she squeaked, 'and I wish we were eating something.' Food comforts all ages in moments of crisis.

One way of coping in bad weather is simply to toss a selection of tins into the pressure cooker, a pot mess stew in fact. The advantage is that it can be added to if the weather continues to be rough. If the weather is bad we usually serve meals in mugs; that way there is a greater chance of the food staying *in situ*. An extremeely simple idea is to make a meal based on Smash. Make up the required amount of instant potato and add a tin of spinach, or tomatoes, or anything you fancy, together with one or two eggs and perhaps a little cheese. This makes a very simple but warm, filling meal that will not upset delicate stomachs; being fairly solid in texture it is unlikely to spill. Another idea is to resort to toasted sandwiches.

CHAPTER NINE

The First-Aid Box

The RYA have published an excellent booklet on first aid which covers almost every eventuality, except childbirth. (*Reed's Nautical Almanac* still has the instructions about boiling pieces of string, etc.) This book should be carried on board every yacht. For serious offshore passages it is worth taking a look at the *The International Code of Radio Signals*. This publication covers all the flag and Morse code signals for every eventuality from distress and emergency, navigation and manoeuvres, to communications, meteorological and medical advice. Apart from the serious and practical angle, this book provides enormous scope for the crew to put together any number of unlikely messages. We have been known to greet our friends in an anchorage flying the following flags: XP, JW, VQ O, NC, JD 4. Which roughly translated means: 'I am stopped in a thick fog, with a leak and no ice, we require assistance and there is danger of toxic effects.' There are many more signals which when used in unlikely combinations can have hilarious, if rather vulgar translations.

As to what to take in the way of first aid, your local pharmacist will be able to help you with suggestions of what to carry in your first-aid box. There will be some items, such as antibiotics, for which a prescription is needed and which your GP will write for you when you explain where and for how long you expect to be cruising. It is worth remembering to ask the pharmacist to label each bottle with not only the name and dosage but also the use of the drug. I once delivered a yacht owned by an anaesthetist. His first-aid boxes were crammed full of an exciting array of ampoules, hypodermic syringes and many interesting-looking gadgets, none of which meant anything to me. I think he could have carried out a full brain transplant, but if I had wanted an aspirin, I would not have known where to find it.

It is a good idea to have two or three first-aid boxes clearly labelled on the outside and include a list of contents inside. The crew should know where they are kept, the heads, for example, where they can easily be got at, and not buried deep in the bottom of a locker. We find it easiest to package the treatments for various parts of the body in individual plastic bags inside the boxes so that all the eye treatments are together in one bag, stomach complaints in another, and so on. All treatments for external use are in one box, internal in another. This helps to avoid confusion in the event of an emergency. Happily the medicine chest is not raided too often, except for the usual hangover cures, so it is very easy to forget to check it over and replace what has been used up in the course of a season. In the golden days of J-Class racing the medicine chests were topped up after each day's racing.

It is also worth finding out if any of the crew is allergic to penicillin. (He or she should in any case carry an alternative of their own.) If any member of the crew suffers from any kind of chronic illness, diabetes, heart trouble or asthma, for example, it is vital that the skipper is aware of this and ensures that they have sufficient supplies of their medicines with them if planning a protracted cruise in an isolated region.

Here are some suggestions for inclusion in your first-aid box:

EXTERNAL USE – Dressings and bandages

Cut and grazes
  Antiseptic wipes
  Bandages, assorted sizes
  Cotton wool
  Elastic bandages, assorted sizes
  Eye pads
  Finger stalls
  Large wound dressings
  Medium wound dressings
  Safety pins
  Scissors
  Sterile gauze swabs
  Sterile suture strips
  Surgical tape
  Triangular bandage

Tweezers, for removing splinters, etc.
Waterproof adhesive dressings, assorted sizes
Burns
　Aerosol burn spray
　Medicated burn dressings
Eyes
　Optrex and eye bath, *or* solution of warm salt water and eggcup
　eye bath
　Eye ointment for conjunctivitis
Sunburn
　Solarcaine aerosol spray for relief of sunburn
　Caladryl cream for sunburn and itching skin
　Total block lip salve
　Waterproof sun screen, high factor
Skin
　Tinaderm powder for athlete's foot
　Vaseline for lubricant and chapped skin
　Lanolin
Bruises
　Arnica cream (homoeopathic)
　Calendula when skin is broken
Insect stings and bites
　Autun, or any insect repellent
　Solarcaine, cream or spray, stops the itching
　Caladryl cream, for itching skin
Water
　Purification tablets for the main water tanks
　Filter. The Hospital for Tropical Diseases sells a small filter kit

INTERNAL USE
(These do not require a prescription in the UK)

Bruises and swelling
　Soluble aspirin
Constipation
　Be sure that you can attribute constipation to natural causes.
　Senokot tablets within 36 hrs
Dehydration
　From excessive heat, seasickness, or diarrhoea

Electrolyte/glucose product such as Re-Hidrat.
The same solution can be made by dissolving 1 dessertspoon of
sugar or honey and a pinch of salt in 300 ml (1/2/pt) of water
Diarrhoea
Arrèt, acts within 2 hrs
Indigestion
Aludrox tablets
Insect bites and stings
Antihistamine tablets (Piriton)
Moderate pain
Paracetamol (analgesic)
Muscular pain
Ibuprufen
Seasickness
Stugeron – preventive
Kwells – for actual seasickness
Stomach upsets, mild
No food and plenty of liquids (not milk), but should symptoms
persist for more than 36 hrs seek medical advice
Tooth injuries
Zinc oxide dressing
Toothache
Oil of cloves. Corsodyl is good for most mouth troubles.

SEASICKNESS

Treatment before departure – The company who can come up
with a cure that prevents seasickness without any side-effects would
endear itself for ever to sailors all over the world. Everyone has an
individual cure, ranging from acupressure pads to pills and potions,
from nibbling ginger biscuits and drinking tonic water to, for all I
know, magical remedies boiled up by a witch doctor by the light of
the new moon.

Stugeron appears by all accounts to be the most effective preventive.
The most common mistake is not taking Stugeron until you are
actually feeling queasy. As it is a preventive it must be taken well
before the outset of the passage, which may be at least 2–3 hours,
but if you know that you are a chronic sufferer, try taking it at least
24–36 hours ahead of departure. Prevention is better than cure.

Most people are well aware that eating and drinking in moderation prior to departure is good common sense, but advice that is sometimes ignored to your cost when, two hours out of Deauville, you have instant recall of a delicious and exotic lunch washed down by Calvados, in bumpers.

Treatment at sea – For the first few days at sea, plainly cooked food that is easily digested. It is far better to design your meals round a kettle and quickly prepared snacks instead of struggling to produce a three-course meal, as one green face can infect the whole crew. There is enough nourishment to be had from bread and cheese or a handful of nuts and raisins if that is all you can manage to produce without rushing to the lee rail. As some people find the smell of any frying nauseous, steer clear of the pan and have grilled bacon sandwiches instead. Porridge is good solid fodder, especially with a dollop of honey. Some people find that they cannot drink coffee at all, and for some reason they find that white coffee is worse than black. Avoid bringing out the kippers until the crew have found their sea-legs.

Most people recover from seasickness after two or three days at sea; some suffer more than others and if the weather is rough may be affected for up to five days. During the Round Britain Race, where we had five compulsory stopovers, the real heroes were those who had just recovered from being sick, when they had to set off and go to sea again. Being sick is bad enough, retching on an empty stomach even worse; it is better to nibble on a dry biscuit than retch on an empty stomach. Encourage the patient to suck a barley sugar as he will benefit from the glucose. Seasickness is rarely dangerous in itself except in extreme cases when the sufferer may become dehydrated; constant sips of water are better than nothing, but an electrolyte/ glucose product is better, as it will prevent the danger of dehydration in severe cases.

The skipper should keep an eye on a novice crew. Should he notice that they are looking lethargic and yawning frequently, he can be almost certain that they are suffering from the first stages of sickness. In this case, encourage them to take the helm and take an active part because concentrating on the horizon helps, as does the fresh air; if you think that they are past that stage, insist they go below and get into a bunk. Above all do not let them sit in the cockpit getting cold as there is a real danger of hypothermia if a crew member is allowed to sit on deck without wearing waterproofs and warm clothing. Vomiting is associated with sweating, which increases body heat loss. The other danger is the risk of falling overboard when being sick over the lee rail; insist that life harnesses are worn by sick people who are on deck, even in calm weather.

WOUNDS

Not so much about how to cope, but how to avoid.

Imagine a yacht sailing along in a brisk breeze, spinnaker set and the crew lounging around in and around the cockpit. Then think about the positioning of the turning blocks for the sheets and guys. Suppose one of those blocks should break, would anyone be in the direct line of fire? The forces exerted by an exploding block would be sufficient to kill or at the very least maim. Diagram shows the dangerous angle. Beware of any sheet, guy or backstay held in a V by a block. Another hazard is being caught up in the fall of a rope that could suddenly snake round a limb or body, the spinnaker sheet, for example, or any bight in a rope that can suddenly tighten.

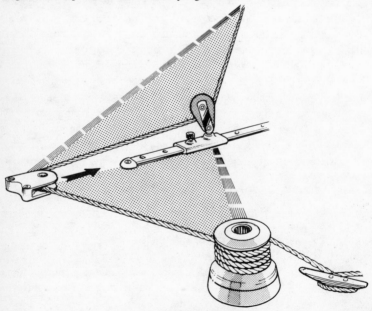

16. Danger angles

I am including this passage from Rob James's *Ocean Sailing* as it is a graphic illustration. They were in the Southern Ocean on the Whitbread Race, 1,000 miles from Tasmania, and had been running fast in strong winds for several days. On the afternoon of 13 November, they decided to take down the storm spinnaker; it was getting very rough.

There were six of us on the foredeck, ready for a forward lower (of the spinnaker). The lazy guy was brought in to the base of the mast and winched in tight until we could get our hands on the leeward corner of the sail. Next I called for the lazy sheet and spinnaker guy to be let go from the inward side. The sail collapsed and flapped forward, partly in the lee of the mainsail. The halyard was eased and the sail fought to the deck. All was safe, and this caused a moment of relaxation at the wrong time, which was nearly fatal. At just that moment we were caught by a wave and knocked beam on to the sea, causing enough heel for our balance to be lost. Part of the spinnaker, or one of its sheets or guys, fell off the foredeck into the water. We were still moving very fast and the sea, rushing past, started to drag the sail out of our grasp and into the water . . .

Nick Dunlop and I rushed to the lee rail just forward of the main shrouds, got our hands on the sail and started to pull. Nick was kneeling and I was standing by his right shoulder. Unfortunately we lost our grip on the cloth and the rest of the sail rushed past us and disappeared astern. It was still attached by five ropes (2 sheets, 2 guys, 1 halyard) and one or more of these had formed a loop on the deck at exactly the point where Nick and I found ourselves. The loop snatched tight as the sail set in the water astern. It was around Nick's waist and my knees, and I think I had a hand caught as well. It pulled tighter and tighter, sinking into Nick's foul-weather gear. My left knee was squeezed by the rope.

I yelled for a knife. Nick was sick and then immediately lost consciousness, his torso hanging limply from the rope loop. We had been dragged down the deck, breaking a stanchion, and were coming up against the rigging. I was still screaming for help when seconds later Ian Worley arrived on the scene and cut every rope in sight – there was so much weight on them, they parted like paper.

They did not have a doctor on board but they were in daily radio contact with one of the other yachts in the race who did. They altered course for Hobart and when, four days later, it became clear that Nick had recovered, they were able to alter course and resume racing.

HANGOVERS

Many people have their own patent cure for hangovers, but the only thing that works, as I'm sure everyone is perfectly aware, is to avoid over-indulgence in the first place. We all know that the path of good intentions leads to Hell, but it still does not stop us tippling down that primrose road once in a while. When the morning after is remarkable only for its brightness, and toast being chewed sounds like the 1812 *Overture* being played in quadrophonic sound, either retire to bed or go for a good long swim. Some people swear by Fernet Branca, others by prairie oysters; my advice is to drink as much water as possible, two pints at least with an aspirin before adopting a horizontal position. Alcohol is very dehydrating, which is why copious amounts of water may help the poor beleaguered liver in its battle to throw off the poison. Fresh air and exercise also help to get it out of your system. A mild case can be corrected by the hair of the dog, say a Horse's Neck (brandy and ginger ale) or a Buck's Fizz (champagne and orange juice). But beware of over-correcting.

TOOTHACHE AND OTHER MOUTH TROUBLES

A visit to the dentist is a wise precaution to take before any cruise and could save you hours of pain and misery. Toothache is almost as bad and severe as earache, some would say worse. Oil of cloves can help as it acts as an anaesthetic; chewing a whole clove will have the same effect. Severe pain, an abscess under a tooth, for example, can be held at bay by chewing codeine tablets on the tooth. I was told by a navigator of a submarine that he once held down an impacted wisdom tooth with an abscess under it for thirty-four days: it was either that or succumb to the coxswain's pliers. Corsodyl helps to soothe ulcers, abscesses and other mouth troubles. On a long cruise you should prescribe a course of antibiotics for an abscess.

UPSET STOMACHS

Stomach upsets, the 'trots', usually affect people in hot climates, especially in those parts of the world where the standards of hygiene are a bit suspect. Old India hands in the days of the Empire would have told you that precaution number one was not to eat any salad or fruit at all. Luckily there is no need to take such an extreme view today *provided* all salads, vegetables and fruit are thoroughly washed in clean, fresh water. If you want to be extra certain, when sailing with very small children, for example, dissolve some permanganate of potash in the water and peel all fruit. Another common cause is the ice cubes in your drinks ashore where you cannot be sure of the source of the water. Always drink bottled water rather than having a jug on the table, and in some countries ice-creams sold on street corners have been known to be suspect. The recommended treatment for stomach upsets today is to put the patient on a starvation diet and to see that they drink as much sugar and salt liquid as possible. If the symptoms have not stopped after 36 hours then there is a chance that there is an infection and medical advice should be sought.

When the pale-faced crew arrive from the cool climate of England encourage them not to sit out in the midday sun until they have become acclimatized to the heat, as this often causes trouble. Too much food and drink in the heat can also produce unpleasant symptoms. Years ago, whatever the problem was, everyone resorted to Dr J Collis Browne's magical compound for mountaineers, which is no longer available in its original form because of its high content of addictive drugs like laudanum and opium. Fifty-fifty port and brandy is not a bad substitute.

DANGERS FROM FISH

Ciguatera

The most prevalent type of seafood poisoning throughout the tropics, ciguatera, is caused by the heat-stable toxin known as ciguatoxin, which is produced by free-swimming, single-celled marine organisms classified as dinoflagellates. These creatures attach themselves to algae at the bottom of the food chain and are passed up it through fish of a variety of sizes and species. Hundreds of different types of fish in tropical and subtropical waters can be affected.

Dr Raymond Bagnis, head of the Medical Oceanographic Research Unit at the Louis Mallarde Institute in Tahiti and a leading authority on ciguatera, has shown that outbreaks of this phenomenon have followed one or two years after some major disturbance or damage to a coral reef.

For reasons not fully understood, fish carrying the toxin are not in themselves affected by it nor are the bigger fish that eat them. Only when man eats such a fish does the toxin become apparent by the potentially fatal illness it causes. There is no way of telling whether a fish is infected or not; even more sinister, the toxin is not destroyed by freezing or cooking. Dr Bagnis's advice is never to eat larger fish, and to fillet all fish regardless of size as it is believed that greater concentrations of the toxins will be found against the backbone. He also recommends feeding a portion of fish to the ship's cat a few hours before preparation. He has never suffered from ciguatera – but then neither has the cat.

Fish caught off soundings are seldom contaminated, especially such truly pelagic species as tuna, dorado and marlin, a fact that makes eating fish during ocean passage relatively safe.

Symptoms of ciguatera include nausea, vomiting, stomach-cramps and diarrhoea. Ciguatera toxin is capable of lodging against the stomach lining where it causes no harm until dislodged by the consumption of more contaminated flesh or excess alcohol.

Note that this terrifying bug will not be found in temperate or cold waters.

Sea Urchins

These black-spined creatures litter rocky coastlines in warm waters. If trodden on, the spines penetrate the foot and break off. They are difficult to remove. Beware of secondary infections.

The easiest way to avoid being stung or stabbed by any of these creatures is to take the simple precaution of wearing sandals or shoes when swimming.

Great Weever

This is a dangerous fish as the venom injected produces instant pain which spreads to all parts of the body. There is no known antidote. Its habitat ranges from the Mediterranean to southern Norway; it is very rare to come across one in UK waters, although a child was stung by one in Wales in 1988.

Stingrays

Quite common in the Mediterranean. They lie half buried under the sand in the shallows. If trodden on by mistake the stingray lashes out with its tail and stabs a spine into your foot. Very painful.

Octopus

A much maligned creature that is much more frightened of you.

Jelly fish

Most of these creatures sting, but apart from the Portuguese Man-of-War, few are dangerous. Be careful when pulling up anchor chains in jelly-fish infested waters as tentacles can stick to the chain and will still sting. Wear gloves, and, if stung, an antihistamine cream will help. If severely stung, seek medical advice.

CHAPTER TEN

Some Foreign and Regional Foods

Gastronomy is the joy of every condition and every age. It adds beauty to wit. Ponder well on this point: the pleasant hours of our life are all connected, by a more or less intangible link, with some memory of the table.

Monselet, *Larousse Gastronomique*

One of the joys of cruising foreign parts is sampling the local cuisine and tasting the beverages of the area. This chapter is a brief introduction to a few of the regional dishes that you can find along the coastline of the North Atlantic.

A total stranger could be forgiven if he expressed the opinion that there is little variation in cooking from Belgium to the Basque country. In a way he may not be far wrong, especially if he has only eaten his way south at harbour-side cafés; *Moules Marinière* is as indigenous to coastal France as fish and chips are to England; the only variation is how well or badly cooked they are. The secret is not to fall into the obvious tourist-trap restaurant overlooking the harbour, but to find instead an eatery with atmosphere and good, reasonably priced fare which may be a little farther back in the town.

There are still plenty of places in France that are family-run and very much part of the local community. I remember one such place at the mouth of the Loire. After a morning's refuelling and shopping, and in urgent need of liquid refreshment, we fell into the first bar. It was packed with the local gendarmerie, *sapeurs pompier, et al.* Promptly at 1230, Madame threw wide the double doors at the back of the room and announced '*est servi*'. Although we hadn't planned on eating lunch ashore, we found ourselves seated at a long table with the rest of the village eating one of the finest meals ever.

HOLLAND

The migrant communities of the Dutch East Indies have had a major influence on Dutch cooking, bringing with them the taste for hot and spicy food. Nasi Goreng and Rijsttafel are considered just as much a national dish as the traditional herrings, eels, and pea soup. Rijsttafel is the most famous Indonesian dish and takes its name from the Dutch word meaning a rice-table. It is usually served buffet-style: a huge bowl of rice and many different side dishes to help yourself to, ranging from mildly spicy to some which are positively incandescent. As a very broad rule of thumb, the beef and lamb dishes tend to be hotter than chicken, fish, and vegetable ones.

'Haring in't land, dokter aan de kant' – loosely translated means 'A herring a day keeps the doctor away'. The famous raw herring beloved of the Dutch may not be to everyone's taste, but should be tried at least once; quantities of Bols Jenever Gin help wash it down.

Smoked eels are delicious. Eat them with brown bread and butter, a squeeze of lemon and black pepper. They can be bought vacuum-packed so keep for quite a long time. Freshwater-eel stew is another delicacy well worth trying when in Holland.

BELGIUM

The Belgians are so fond of *frites* that, according to one national newspaper, they have opened a museum in Antwerp devoted entirely to the fried potato. Belgian cuisine is essentially Flemish, but there is little difference between the cooking style of Flanders, in the south, and the Netherlands, in the north; yet it does have a peculiar character of its own. Real Ostend fish soup is a meal in itself. Many years ago fishermen mounted on vast cart-horses sploshed up and down the beach in pursuit of their prey, the tiny grey shrimp. They have long since abandoned this unusual method of fishing, although the shrimps are just as popular, served with sliced tomatoes and mayonnaise. You may find on the menu rabbit or beef cooked in beer, which are worth trying. The Belgians are justly famous for their chocolate, which is totally irresistible for chocoholics.

NORMANDY

The chalk plain that stretches across the northern part of Normandy to the Seine is covered by a thick layer of rich loamy soil and, together with the mild weather, provides the ideal conditions for dairy pasture. Normandy is justly famous for her panda-eyed cattle which produce the rich thick cream to make the cheeses of the area. If you find yourself in Boulogne, don't depart before a visit to probably the most famous cheese shop in France: Philippe Olivier in Rue Thiers is a veritable Aladdin's cave of cheese. He sells his own Camembert, labelled Olivier, which is the best you will find anywhere. He doesn't buy cheese from the factories but from farmers and small local producers, then matures them himself. Maroilles, an orange-coloured cheese with a wonderful nutty flavour, must be double-wrapped or your boat will be almost untenable.

Someone confided in me that he was having terrible trouble with his co-owner. Apparently it was quite normal for them to leave their clean clothes on board, but this year his partner had taken to leaving his dirty ones too, and the smell of unwashed socks was appalling. 'I've gently hinted to him about the pong but he accuses me, and says it's my socks, not his.' They both took their clothes home the following weekend, but when I joined them a couple of weeks later, there was still a definite something in the air, so to speak. We searched the boat from stem to stern in an effort to find the source of the evil smell, with no success. When they laid the boat up for the winter they discovered, jammed under the bilges, a partly disintegrated box with Camembert barely discernible on the lid. It was given a ceremonial burial.

Livarot is a Normandy cheese with a highly developed smell and with a full flavour. Pont-l'Evêque has a strong smell, but the taste is mellow with a slight bite to it. The origins of Brie are ancient and are thought to date as far back as Roman times; it was certainly being made in the reign of Charlemagne. There are six authentic French Brie, and many imitations. Other cheeses of the region include Neufchâtel, Bondon and Gournay as well as local goats' cheeses.

A distinctive feature of a large number of the Normandy dishes is that they are cooked in cream. Any fish dish that is described as *à la Normande* is braised in white wine and served with a creamy sauce garnished with mussels, shrimps and mushrooms; *à la Dieppoise* is much the same, although the fish should be poached in fish stock and garnished with grey or pink shrimps, and shelled mussels cooked in wine, and coated with a white sauce.

Calvados is the famous apple brandy of the region. Well matured it is as smooth as silk, but the cheaper brands have a powerful enough kick to launch a missile. Drink it on its own or use for cooking with port, duck and apples. It is well worth buying some to take home. Try a little poured over a lime sorbet.

Other regional dishes include plump ducks from Rouen and Duclair, *tripes à la môde de Caen* and the pork products such as *boudin blanc* (white sausages).

BRITTANY

The coast of north Brittany is said to be the vegetable garden of France. The soil itself is not as naturally fertile as that of Normandy, but for generations they have ploughed in marle (crushed seashells) which, like seaweed, is rich in phosphates and other minerals.

Legions of grey-green artichokes march across the horizon followed by leeks, onions, cabbages and sprouts. The coastal waters are a minefield of lobster and crab pots waiting to catch the unwary yacht's propeller, and the forest of stakes in the mouths of the rivers reveal acres of mussel and oyster beds at low water.

Brittany seafood is some of the finest anywhere in the world, from the tiny grey shrimps to the famous Belon oysters. Clams, mussels, crabs, winkles, lobster and langoustine make up a plate of *fruits de mer*. Tuna and sardines are local specialities from Brest to Belle-Île.

Lamb that has grazed on the salt meadows served *à la Bretonne* with beans is a speciality, as are the fat black sausages from Quimper. Buckwheat pancakes with any amount of assorted fillings are popular with young and old alike. In any supermarket you can buy packets of ready-made crêpes which only need warming through and stuffing with your own filling to make an excellent meal; it is worth buying some to take home. Breton cakes and especially their rich buttery biscuits are delicious.

A good bottle of well-chilled *cidre bouché* is hard to beat – it is also more alcoholic than you think, as we discovered a few years ago when the senior daughter was seen weaving her way through the anchorage singing a surprisingly bawdy song for one of such tender years. Muscadet and Gros Plant are the local wines and are perfect to wash down a plate of *fruits de mer*. Go for Muscadet-sur-Lie where possible. It has been matured in casks with the grapeskins and stalks still there.

Further south towards La Rochelle you will find that fresh tuna is more frequently on the menu and if you are in luck, you might also find goose barnacles, known as *pouce-pied*. When they are served cold with mayonnaise, I can only describe their taste as an amalgamation of shellfish. On market day, when the squares are packed with stalls, you may witness a macabre dance as handfuls of young live eels are thrown on to a charcoal grill to roast to a snappy brown while knots of hungry shoppers look on as they wait to munch these tender morsels.

SPAIN – North Atlantic coast

Fish and shellfish of all kinds abound along the Spanish coast, and are usually fried in oil. *Mariscos* (Spanish for *fruits de mer*) are a highlight of La Coruña. Every country has its own version of fish stew. The Spanish *caldereta* is the equivalent of the Provençal *bouilla-baisse*, the *bulavesa* of the Spanish Mediterranean coast and the *caldei-rada* of Portugal. The most common cooking utensil in Spain is the brown earthenware open casserole. It is a most attractive and useful vessel as it can be used on the top of the cooker (with care) as well as in the oven; secrete a few on board, well wrapped in paper, to take home as presents. Large stuffed squid and octopus bathed in a rich and inky black sauce are wonderful when well prepared. Although it is not difficult to cook and prepare, I would rather not tackle a live octopus on board a boat, or anywhere else for that matter. You will find that everything is fried in olive oil, which some people find too heavy.

PORTUGAL

Portuguese olive oil has a most distinctive taste as the olives are kept in store for a week before being pressed. Elsewhere, they are pressed almost immediately. *Calamares* (squid), *baccalhau* (dried salt cod), charcoal-grilled sardines and hake (*pescada*) are among the most popular items on the menu.

AZORES

These islands are Portuguese and the cooking is similar. The locally produced red wine, dark purple in colour, is fairly powerful; it does not travel well as we have discovered to our cost. Local pineapples and bananas are plentiful and are certainly worth taking on board. There are supermarkets, but they are quite expensive.

CANARIES

The influence on the cooking here is mainly Spanish, as you would expect. The supermarkets are well stocked with a wide variety of everything. Spirits and wine are very cheap. The markets are full of good fresh vegetables and fruit; the best place to store up for the trade-wind dash across to the West Indies. Avoid the commercial harbours like Las Palmas or Santa Cruz; instead try Puerto Rico or Placito Blanco in the south of Gran Canarias.

CARIBBEAN

Into a vast cauldron (or the pressure cooker) throw ghee and masala paste from India, sweet peppers and tomatoes from Spain, French salt cod, Chinese water chestnuts, a haggis from Scotland, add a jigger of rum, stir and season to taste. Savour, a sip at a time, and gradually the panorama of Caribbean cookery will unfold before your palate.

Caribbean cookery is above all an eclectic mix of ingredients and cooking methods from all over Europe, Asia and Africa. Each island has its own specialities, depending on who conquered it last. As the islanders travel they take with them their individual recipes which then are adapted further according to what is available on other islands. Some islands have pigs and some do not, but all have coconut and banana desserts in common. The culinary influences at work are legion, but if you divide the islands into language groups, then it is easier to distinguish the characteristic styles of cooking. In the Spanish-speaking islands, *sofrito* is a pungent sweet pepper and tomato sauce. In Trinidad, where there is a strong Indian influence, masala, a curry paste or powder and ghee (clarified butter) are widely used. A strong French influence is apparent in the use of herbs and spices in the islands that changed hands innumerable times between the British and French. Martinique and Guadaloupe offer the best French wines available in the islands.

CHAPTER ELEVEN

Fish and Shellfish

Trailing a line astern in the hopes of catching a mackerel for supper is a traditional pastime enjoyed by many. This is fine so long as you don't mind catching something you didn't bargain for, like garfish, for example. These weird-looking creatures look like miniature swordfish with a beak up to three inches long, armoured with rows of vicious teeth; their flesh, which some people consider a delicacy, is a phosphorescent green. You know when you have caught one, as their eel-like silvery bodies rise whirling and thrashing to the surface, teeth snapping in rage. This is the moment when, coward as I am, I dive for cover leaving someone else to handle the situation. If you are not that successful at fishing yourself there are always the fish markets to visit, especially when cruising in France. Around five every evening the *criée* takes place at the fishing ports. It is a fascinating spectacle, the porters unloading the crates of glittering fish, which are then weighed, auctioned and packed into waiting lorries. The whole process takes little more than an hour. Stalls are set up along the quayside and housewives jostle and bargain for transluscent pink langoustine and fierce-looking crabs. This is the place to buy your supper at the best prices.

When I was young we spent our holidays in Polruan, a small village in Cornwall on the opposite side of the river from Fowey. As well as being taught to sail by a remarkable local character, Walter Brennan, we were also taught to fish. There was one instruction that completely mystified me: on no account were we to mention rabbits and, if we did, he would put back. In spite of constant pressure to explain, Walter would simply shake his head and say, ' 'Tis bad luck, my dear.' When I mentioned this to someone recently, he remarked that he sails with a friend who firmly believes that mentioning rabbits inevitably brings three disasters in a row: a dismasting, a rope round the screw, and a grounding on the ebb. You have been warned.

Mackerel are ocean fish which swim in very large shoals. They have a long spawning season that brings them into the shallow waters of the Continental shelf from spring to late summer. They are voracious feeders and grab at anything. The simplest method of catching them is to use a spinner at the end of a long length of nylon, connected at either end by swivels on to the weight which is joined with another swivel on to the line, thus preventing the whole caboodle twisting up in knots. Maintaining the correct speed is vital to success when trawling for mackerel, neither too fast nor too slow, the ideal speed being somewhere between 2–3 knots under way; or arrange to kedge off somewhere like the Cherbourg peninsula where the stream runs somewhere between 3–4 knots. If under way, don't forget that the faster your speed, the heavier the weight and the longer the length of line has to be to keep the spinner deep enough. The best times of day are either dawn or dusk, especially at the height of the summer when the midday light is diamond bright and no fish will rise, as any fisherman will tell you. Damp, misty days are good, too.

You may be lucky and catch a fish in mid Channel, but ideally you don't want to be further than a couple of miles off shore. When fishing under way it is best to secure the line off on a guardrail stanchion rather than a cleat on the quarter; that way there is less chance of catching the propeller. Serious foul-ups usually occur when the helmsman tacks without warning, and the line wraps itself smartly round the propeller or rudder. Brownie points will be deducted for this manoeuvre.

Round fish: Different techniques are called for when it comes to cooking round fish, for example, pollack, grey mullet, herring and mackerel. Mackerel needs little preparation apart from gutting. Other round fish must have their hard, coarse scales removed. This is not easy to do on board as the scales tend to fly into the most unlikely places even if you have taken every precaution by covering the galley in newspaper.

To remove the scales: using a damp cloth for grip, hold the fish firmly by the tail and with the back of a strong knife remove the scales by pushing them up the wrong way from tail to head. If you are buying a coarse-scaled fish from a market, the stallholder will do this for you if you ask him.

To gut the fish: slit the fish open from the vent near its tail up towards its head. Remove the guts and gills. Wash in clean salt water.

To remove the backbone: having caught your mackerel, make sure they are laid out straight to stiffen and are not left curled in a bucket. Cut the fish from the vent towards the tail, sliding the knife as close to the bone as possible. Remove the head and tail. Lay the fish flat on a board, cut side down, and press along the backbone to loosen it. Turn the fish over and lift out the backbone and any other small bones which may be sticking out. If the fish is large, a salmon for example, you may need to use a pair of pliers to remove the bones. Cut the backbone off at each end using scissors or a knife. Left whole, the fish is now ready for stuffing or it can be filleted by cutting along the top of the backbone and lifting the top fillet right off. They can be sautéd in butter which, although very rich, is the best way. To grill, make a couple of diagonal slashes on either side and grill for about five minutes, turn and grill for a further five minutes, depending on size.

Flat fish such as sole or plaice need different treatment.

To skin and fillet the fish: using a sharp knife, make a cut down each side of the fish between the fins and the flesh. Loosen the skin by running the thumb under the flap of the skin. Ease the skin away from the flesh at the tail end and then, with your fingers, pull quickly from tail to head, removing the skin completely. Still using a sharp knife, cut the fish down the centre backbone, which is clearly visible. Working from the head and keeping the knife close to the bone, cut in sweeping strokes from the right to the left until the fillet is lifted. Turn the fish round and do the same on the other side and then repeat on the reverse side of the fish until you have four fillets in all.

Mussels: As the tide falls from the rock-strewn shore, people armed with buckets and plastic bags descend to forage among the fronds of seaweed for a meal there for the picking. Clumps of blue-black mussels cling to the rocks, and shiny black winkles are found close by. Some sandy beaches yield cockles and razorshells as well. You can see men, women and children, armed with blunt-nosed shrimping nets, wading knee deep along the edge of the beach, every one of them intent on gathering a free dinner.

Make sure that you pick your mussels, or any other crustacean for that matter, only from a clean and unpolluted area. If the mussels have come from a sandy place let them soak in several changes of fresh salt water to expel the sand. Do not leave them to soak overnight in fresh water as this kills them. To clean, pull off their 'whiskers', scrub thoroughly and remove any barnacles by scraping them off using the back of an old knife. Any mussel that does not shut when tapped sharply should be jettisoned. To cook, see recipes on pages 119 and 120.

Cockles: these are usually found in river estuaries and on shallow sandy beaches at the bottom of the tide. They lie half buried in the sand and are not easy to see at first. You may see professional cockle-pickers striding along the beach armed with a garden rake, which they use to scrape the shells up from the sand. It would be a little cumbersome, not to say impracticable to carry a full-size rake on board, but a children's rake, of the type often used for making sand-castles, is a much better idea. Cockles, due to their habitat, do need soaking in several changes of fresh salt water to rid them of their sand. They can be eaten raw with a squeeze of lemon juice, in soup to make a chowder, or best of all with butter, garlic and spaghetti.

Winkles (*bigorneaux*): one of the most common molluscs found on rocky beaches. They usually play second fiddle to the exotic shellfish that make up a plate of *fruits de mer*. They are easily recognizable by their small black shells that have a sharp point on the top. Boil for about ten minutes in *court bouillon* with a bay leaf. Use a 'winkle-picker' or hat pin to flick off their lids and then prise the little creature out of his shell.

Oysters: 'It's a wery remarkable circumstance, sir,' said Sam Weller in *Pickwick Papers*, 'that poverty and oysters always seem to go together.' Unfortunately for oyster lovers, this is no longer true. Oysters from Cancale, St Vaast and the Belon and Auray rivers are famous for their delicate flavour and well worth a diversion, as the *Guide Michelin* says.

To open: hold the oyster firmly in one hand, flat side up, with the hinge pointing away from you. Holding a broad-bladed, strong knife in the other hand, insert the point at the hinge and push firmly into the oyster. Then slide the knife around either side of the shell and lift off the top half of the shell. Some people like them with just a squeeze of lemon juice, others like a dash of tabasco sauce as well. In Brittany they usually serve them with a dip of vinegar and chopped shallots, rather than lemons. Whichever way you like to eat them, a good Muscadet-sur-Lie or a green Gros Plant are excellent wines to accompany them.

Crabs: (*tourteaux* or flat-backed): there is some dispute as to which is the kindest way to kill lobsters and crabs. One way is to plunge them into boiling water and the other is to put them into cold water and bring them to the boil. If you don't fancy cooking them yourself, buy them ready cooked. Bring a large pot of salted water to the boil, drop in the crab and cover with a lid and simmer for twenty minutes; allow to cool in the water.

When cold, turn the crab on to its back, twist off the small legs and large claws and set aside. Push back the tail flap and twist off. Holding the crab firmly with one hand, hook your thumb and first finger of the other hand into the holes left by the claws and pull the body of the crab away from its shell. Remove and discard the gills or 'dead men's fingers'.

The mouth and stomach sac are situated in the top of the shell just below the eyes. Press down on the mouth with your thumb and lift this and the sac out and discard. That is the easy part of the task. Cut the body of the crab into two and pick out all the white flesh from the cavities. A skewer or small pick is the ideal implement. (I do not advise that you purloin the navigator's dividers without his consent). Crack open the large claws with a winch-handle; a pair of pliers will do for the smaller legs.

Using a teaspoon, scrape out all the brown meat into a separate bowl. If you study the underside of the carapace, you will see a natural line around the edge. Press firmly down along the line and it will break away, giving a much larger space in which to pile the white and brown meat back in the middle. A fresh crab salad is to my way of thinking one of the finest meals and should be served simply with some home-made mayonnaise, bread and wine. In the tropics crabs are served with strips of ripe mango: the two flavours complement each other to perfection.

Spider Crab: cook and open in the same way as the flat-backed crab, although you may have more problems fitting the long legs into a saucepan. The body is rather harder to separate from the shell and there is little brown meat. The white flesh is firm and sweet.

Lobster: when boiled, it is as red as a cardinal's hat! Expensive on both sides of the Atlantic, but a rare treat. To cook, drop into rapidly boiling water, simmer for 20–30 minutes and allow to cool in the water. When cold, lay the lobster on its back and split the body in half. Remove the stomach and the dark thread of intestine. All the rest is edible, including the dark green bit which many ignore.

Langoustine: they are sometimes known as Dublin Bay prawns but according to Alan Davidson's catalogue of North Atlantic seafood, they are not, in fact, an inhabitant of Dublin Bay. Apparently this misnomer occurred because fishing boats calling into Dublin often had these prawns on board. Either cook them in a *court bouillon*, or in well-salted water for ten minutes, drain and leave to cool. Serve them cold with mayonnaise or hot, sautéd in olive oil and garlic and flamed in brandy; they are wonderful hot or cold served in a mild curry sauce.

Scallops: the deeply-ridged, fan-shaped shellfish range in size from large to the quite small ones called 'queens' in America. They are usually cleaned at sea and come ashore to be sold with only their muscle and orange-coloured roe. If you buy them uncleaned, remove the frill of eyes before poaching or grilling them.

Clams: they are a vast family that range from the huge Quahog, to the smaller Littleneck and Cherrystone clams from North America. The Quahog has been introduced here and are farmed in the Helford River and at Newport on the Isle of Wight. In France you will find Palourdes and Prairies on the menu. Clams can be served in chowders, or simply steamed open and served on the half shell with butter.

Goose-neck barnacles (*Pouce-pied*): these extraordinary looking creatures grow in clumps on rocks of the south coast of southern Brittany, Spain and Portugal. I am not sure if they are the same as the white goose-neck barnacle that grows on the bottom of long-distance yachts and looks like toothpaste or macaroni. They are easily recognizable by their finger-thick tube of dark scaly skin and the top looks exactly like a kind of bony hoof. I first came across them when we were at La Rochelle and were shown by a friendly French boat where to look for them. Having prised them off the rocks, simply boil briefly in salt water, pinch off the outer skin near the hoofs to reveal a juicy pink stalk which you eat whole. The taste is a revelation.

Flying fish: the first time you see these lovely creatures skitter and glide across the waves you know you can honestly call yourself a blue water sailor. It can be quite spooky if you are alone on deck at night watching the stars wheel overhead and suddenly be thumped between the shoulder blades. Jumping out of your skin with fright, you shout,

'Who's that?' turning round and half expecting to see a bearded desperado with a knife between his teeth standing on the pushpit. Instead, the only midnight visitor is a flying fish that has crash-landed. On a good morning you may find three or four on deck. The bigger ones make very good eating. Cut off the wings and other appendages with galley scissors, split open and remove backbone. Then sauté them in butter.

Fish in the West Indies, especially those caught near coral reefs, may harbour the dreaded ciguatoxin (see page 85). But those caught off-soundings or in temperate and cold waters are rarely contaminated.

CHAPTER TWELVE

Recipes – Breakfast

There was an old man from Thermopylae
Who never did anything properly;
But they said, 'If you choose
To boil eggs in your shoes,
You shall never remain in Thermopylae.'
Edward Lear,
One Hundred Nonsense Pictures and Rhymes

Corncakes   Serves 4

The mixture can be pre-made at home as it needs time to mature
before cooking. It is also easy to make on board in all but the worst
conditions. Corncakes absorb a lot of butter while they are cooking,
so be sure to drain well on kitchen towels before serving.

85g (3oz) plain flour
2 eggs
150ml (5oz) milk
1 tablespoon mashed potato
1 425g (12oz) tin of sweetcorn, drained
340g (4oz) approx. butter

Sift the flour into a bowl and make a well in the centre. Add the eggs
and, using a wooden spoon, mix from the centre, gradually drawing
in the flour from the outer edges. Stir in the milk, beating well until
the batter is smooth and thick. Stir in the drained sweetcorn and the
mashed potatoes. Season with salt and pepper. Put into a screw-top
jar and leave for 24–48 hours.

Melt half the butter in a heavy frying pan and, when foaming, drop
in a couple of spoonfuls of the mixture. Lower the heat a little. When
the cakes are bubbly in the middle and dull at the edges, turn and

fry for a couple more minutes. Remove from the pan and drain on kitchen towels. Keep warm until ready to serve with a rasher or two of bacon and perhaps a fried egg.

Brown Hash   *Serves 4*

There are numerous recipes for this mixture, but this one is highly recommended and can be prepared at home.

> 2 225g (8oz) tins corned beef, mashed with a fork
> 4–6 tablespoons mashed potatoes; you may need more to make it stiff
>   enough
> 1 medium onion, finely chopped
> Lea and Perrins Worcestershire sauce – to taste
> 1–2 teaspoons mustard – to taste
> 1 teaspoon curry powder – to taste
> 1 egg
> butter and oil for frying

Combine all the ingredients in a mixing bowl and add the egg to bind. Divide the mixture into four cakes. Heat the butter and oil in a large frying pan until sizzling, add the cakes two at a time. Lower the heat and cook over a moderate heat until well browned. Turn and cook for a further 5 minutes. Remove, and keep warm. Serve with a fried egg per person.

French Toast   *Serves 2–4*

This is an ideal way of using up stale bread. To be successful it should be made with thick slices of bread that is at least two days old. It can also be prepared and frozen at home, to be taken on board for the weekend.

> 4 thick slices of brown or white bread, crusts trimmed off if feeling classy
> 2 eggs
> 2 tablespoons of milk, or fresh cream
> 2 tablespoons of cold water
> pinch of salt
> generous pinch of cinnamon, more or less to taste
> 110g (4oz) butter

Beat the eggs together with the milk or cream, water, salt and cinnamon. Melt the butter in a heavy frying pan until it is sizzling hot.

While the butter is heating, dip the bread into the egg mixture only long enough to moisten it thoroughly without its becoming totally saturated. Lower the slices into the pan, turning quickly to brown both sides.

Scrambled Anchovy Eggs   *Serves 4*
Scrambled eggs are so quick and easy to do. Serving them on toast spread with anchovy butter makes them a special treat.

    8 eggs
    170g (6oz) butter, unsalted for preference
    2 teaspoons of anchovy paste
    black pepper
    a squeeze of lemon juice
    4 slices of bread

Halve the butter and mix into one half the anchovy paste, pepper and lemon juice and put on one side. Melt the other half in a non-stick saucepan over a low flame. Beat the eggs well and pour into the saucepan, stir frequently until they are just beginning to set. Make the toast and spread thickly with the anchovy butter, but leaving a little butter to stir into the eggs just before they are cooked. Serve the eggs on the anchovy toast.

Oyster Eggs   *Serves 4*
This should be kept as a special treat, your birthday for example.

    8 eggs
    pinch of salt
    pepper
    dash of tabasco sauce, or pinch of chilli powder
    85g (3oz) butter
    1 tin of smoked oysters, drained of oil

Beat the eggs thoroughly with salt, pepper and tabasco. Melt the butter in a non-stick pan over a low flame. Pour in the eggs and stir until they are half cooked. Add the drained oysters and continue cooking until set. Serve with hot toast.

Porridge

Last but not least, don't forget the porridge. It is the best form of ballast known to man, a comfort on cold wet mornings and more likely to stay down than anything else. Fortunately 'instant' oats are easily obtained which reduce the amount of time required to cook the genuine stuff.

Instant porridge is made by stirring boiling milk into a couple of tablespoons per person of the porridge oats.

CHAPTER THIRTEEN

Recipes – Soups

Black Bean Soup   *Serves 4*
While instant soups are quick and easy to prepare, nothing equals a
home-made soup for flavour; this nourishing bean soup is just the
thing to comfort the cockles of your heart especially after a long cold
haul. As this soup is made in a pressure cooker, there is no need to
soak the beans overnight. Black beans can be found in most health
food shops in this country. Do not confuse them with Chinese black
beans which are quite different in flavour.

    500g (1lb) black beans
    2 litres (3½pts) water
    1 ham knuckle bone (optional)
    110g (4oz) lean bacon, diced
    2 medium onions, roughly chopped
    ½ lemon, quarters
    2 sticks celery, including leaves, chopped
    1 large carrot, peeled and roughly chopped
    2 whole cloves
    pinch of allspice
    1 tablespoon salt
    1 glass of sherry
    2 tablespoons sweet red pepper, finely chopped
    2 tablespoons green pepper, finely chopped
    2 tablespoons spring onions, finely chopped

Put the beans into the pressure cooker, cover with cold water and
bring to the boil without covering and simmer for 10 minutes, drain
and discard water. Replace the beans in the cooker and add the 2
litres of water, ham bone or bacon, onions, carrots, celery, cloves and
spice (do not add the salt at this stage). Cover with the lid and bring
to pressure for 30 minutes. Release the pressure slowly. The beans

should be very soft: if not, bring to pressure for a further 10 minutes. Discard the lemon and cloves. If making this at home, put half the soup in a blender and process until smooth. Otherwise put 2 or 3 cups in a bowl and mash with a fork. You may also need to thicken the soup with some mashed potato or cornflour. Return to the pan and heat through, adding sherry and salt to taste. Serve with the peppers and spring onions scattered on the top.

Snert – Dutch green pea soup   *Serves 4–6*
This is a traditional Dutch recipe made from split green peas which do not require soaking overnight. It is a delicious soup that is filling enough to be a meal on its own.

450g (1lb) split green peas
2 litres (3½ pts) water
2 large leeks, cleaned and finely chopped
2 small potatoes, scrubbed and cut into cubes
2 split pig's trotters (optional)
225g (8oz) piece of smoked ham or bacon
3 cloves
1 bayleaf
1 whole smoked sausage
2 teaspoons salt
freshly ground black pepper

Wash the peas and place in a deep saucepan with the water and the rest of the ingredients, except for the sausage and salt. Bring to the boil, then turn down the heat, cover and simmer for about an hour or until the vegetables have become very soft. Remove the trotters and discard. Remove the ham and reserve. Mash the vegetables until smooth. (Blend in a processor if at home.) Cut the ham or bacon into cubes and return to the soup along with the sausage cut into thick slices. Bring up to simmering point and cook for a further 10–15 minutes. Season. Serve with dark rye bread.

Spinach Special   *Serves 4*
Nothing could be easier to prepare than this soup, which is tasty enough to serve up on smart occasions.

300ml (½pt) milk
300ml (½pt) chicken stock, or water and stock cube

400g (140z) tin of spinach purée
a squeeze of lemon, salt and pepper
a pinch of nutmeg

Put the milk and stock into a saucepan and stir in the spinach. Bring to the boil, stirring constantly, reduce the heat and simmer gently for about 5 minutes. Check the seasoning, stir in the nutmeg and lemon juice. Serve with a garnish of *croutons*, and if possible a swirl of cream in each bowl.

Gazpacho   *Serves 6–8*

Unless yours is the sort of yacht that is fully equipped, with a food processor, this soup is difficult to make on board as the vegetables must be puréed with the tomato juice to give it an authentic flavour. If you have the time or energy to chop the vegetables finely by hand, it is just possible to make on board although it will not taste quite the same. Whether it is made on board or at home and transported on board in a thermos flask, it must be served icy cold.

1 450ml (16fl oz) tin or carton of tomato juice
1 small chilli, de-seeded and finely chopped
3–4 cloves of garlic, finely chopped
2 green peppers, de-seeded and quartered
1 red pepper, de-seeded and quartered
1 cucumber, peeled and chopped
2 slices of bread pulled into crumbs
5 tablespoons red wine vinegar
5 tablespoons olive oil
3 tablespoons salt
1 teaspoon sun dried tomato paste
300ml (½pt) water, more if necessary

Garnish
Croutons
3–4 spring onions, finely chopped
½ cucumber, peeled and finely chopped
Ice cubes

At home: Put all the ingredients for the soup into a blender or food processor and blend until fairly smooth. Add the water (you may need a little more) and check the seasoning. Give it a final whiz then chill for a least 2 hours.

On board: Chop the vegetables as finely as possible. Mash the garlic with some of the salt. Combine all the soup ingredients in a bowl and mix thoroughly with your hands. You may not need to add the water as it will not be as thick as when made in a processor. When ready to serve, pour the soup into individual bowls and float a couple of ice cubes on the top. Hand the garnish round separately.

Onion Soup
Serves 6–8

This recipe was immortalized as being that served by Commander E G Martin, founder of the Royal Ocean Racing Club, on his way to winning the first Fastnet Race in his gaff-cutter *Jolie Brise*.

  15 large Spanish onions
  2 tablespoons Bovril
  100g (¼lb) butter
  1 dessertspoon of Worcestershire sauce
  1 wineglass of sherry
  1½ litres (3pts) fresh water

Commander Martin's instructions lead off with: 'First, get someone else to peel and quarter the onions.' Dissolve the Bovril in water and put it in a large saucepan. Stir in the butter, add Worcestershire sauce and sherry; then put the onions in, add water and simmer until all the onions are soft.

CHAPTER FOURTEEN

Recipes – Sandwiches and Bread

Many English people associate sandwiches with soggy triangular affairs filled with something akin to Polyfilla which they might expect to find on trains as a tired apology for a snack. Until I had tasted American sandwiches I had no idea what entirely different creations they could be; a 'club' sandwich is more like a whole meal between bread. By using different types of bread you can add variety of taste and colour. The joy of these is that they freeze beautifully, so long as you avoid using salad or mayonnaise in the fillings, and they keep fresh if well wrapped in cling film and then sealed in plastic bags. They can be fried or grilled, particularly if slightly stale; if frozen they do not need thawing before cooking, which takes only 8 minutes.

Toasted Ham and Cheese Sandwiches   *Serves 4*
This allows for 2 rounds per person. If you want to grill them instead of frying, don't dip in the egg mixture.

    16 slices of brown or white bread, well buttered
    8 thin slices of ham
    8 slices of cheese
    mustard
    1 egg
    1 cup of milk

Spread the bread with butter and mustard and fill with ham and cheese. When ready to serve, beat the egg with the milk and dip each sandwich in the egg mixture and fry for about 4 minutes on either side.

Sandwich Suggestions
These could be made into club sandwiches if you combine three

layers together. Have fun and use your imagination.

Artichoke hearts, cream cheese and garlic
Bacon, fried and served hot
Bully beef mashed with grated Cheddar and mango chutney
Chicken liver and chopped green olives
Chicken, minced and mixed with cream, curry powder, lemon juice and
    tomato purée
Cold roast chicken, cream cheese, olives and mustard pickle
Cream cheese and pineapple
Cream cheese and prawns
Cream cheese, tomato purée and basil sauce
Garlic butter
Pastrami and mustard
Pâté
Rare roast beef with horseradish
Sardines mashed with lots of lemon juice
Smoked salmon pâté
Stilton with grapes
Tinned salmon mixed with horseradish and cream cheese
Tongue with cream cheese mixed with chopped gherkins
Tuna and gherkins

Submarine or Torpedo Sandwiches

Take 1 or 2 French loaves, split and butter both halves. Start at one
end with slices of salami followed by cheese and chutney, scrambled
egg, pâté, chicken mayonnaise, etc., until you have filled the bottom
half with as many different tastes as you want. Replace the top and
wrap in cling film. When ready to eat, cut in two or three and serve
in the wrapping, which is peeled back as you eat your way down the
torpedo.

Dips

Dips served with crisps or raw sticks of vegetables with the evening
drink make a change from the more usual peanuts.

Hummus   *Serves 6*

1 tin of chick peas, drained
2 tablespoons tahini paste
2 cloves of garlic
juice of 1 lemon
oil

fennel seeds

Mash the chick peas with the garlic and beat in the lemon juice and oil until smooth and thick. Season with a little salt and scatter some fennel seeds on the top. If you can find tinned ready-made hummus, it is much improved by the addition of lemon and garlic.

Smoked Cod's Roe – Taramasalata

Make at home for a weekend on board. It does not keep for more than three days.

    55g (2oz) smoked cod's roe, skinned
    2 slices of bread, crusts removed, soaked in water and squeezed dry
    1–2 cloves of garlic
    juice of 1 lemon
    oil

Put the cod's roe in a food processor with the bread and garlic. Blend at high speed for about 30 seconds then pour in the lemon juice. With the machine on, pour in the oil in a steady trickle until the mixture looks like a thick cream.

Smoked Oyster Dip   *Serves 6*

This is good in sandwiches or as a dip with crisps or sticks of *crudités*.

    1 tin of smoked oysters, drained
    225g (8oz) cream cheese
    freshly ground black pepper
    chives
    a little milk or cream

Mash the drained oysters with a fork and mix with the cream cheese, pepper and snipped chives. If it is too thick, thin the mixture with a little milk or cream.

Bread

Cast thy bread upon the waters: for thou shalt find it after many days
                                        (Ecclesiastes 11:1)

The sweet smell of baking bread is finer than all the perfumes of

Arabia. It is guaranteed to revive a moribund crew and certain to endear the maker to everyone. Bill Tilman, the late distinguished mountaineer, sailor and adventurer, was not renowned for providing comfortable cruising conditions. He positively discouraged the crew from buying fresh bread, as he found it far too extravagant, for they always ate the lot at one sitting. But bread is not difficult to make on board and can be baked in a saucepan, pressure cooker or oven. Long-distance cruising people recommend buying whole wheat and grinding it themselves in an old-fashioned type coffee grinder, as ordinary flour gets weevil-infested quickly in the tropics, as mentioned previously. Dried yeast will not last indefinitely; it has a shelf life of about 3–6 months. It is a universal product and can be bought anywhere. There are any number of books devoted entirely to bread-making, but here are a couple of recipes that are easy to make in almost any conditions. I am including a recipe for banana bread as it is not only delicious, but it is also a very good way to use up bananas when too many have ripened at the same time. When making bread with yeast there is only one rule to remember and that is patience: you cannot force the rising process by putting the dough in a warm oven or on the top of radiators, as that may turn the bread sour. The increase of volume is vital; depending on the ambient temperature, it may take anything up to 2 hours.

Stale bread is always much nicer when toasted, which is fine so long as you have a grill. Camping shops sell toasters that are supposed to work on top of the flame. There is one type that looks like a waffle maker in that it consists of two hinged pieces of metal on a handle which you hold over the flame. I have never found it wildly successful. The other Camping-Gaz toaster is a triangular affair that sits on top of the burner and against which you prop two or three pieces of bread. It works quite well so long as it does not fly off the top of the stove. If you are desperate for hot buttered toast and the grill has died, you can always resort to heating the frying pan and browning bread in that, holding it down with a fish slice.

Irish Bread made in a Frying Pan   *Makes 1 loaf*

Nothing could be easier than this bread made in a frying pan. The true Irish version calls for buttermilk, but although it may not be authentic, it still tastes very good made with milk. It must be eaten at once, as it does not keep for long. Variations include adding raisins or caraway seeds.

85g (3oz) butter
680g (1½lb) flour
1½ teaspoons salt
1 tablespoon baking powder
170g (6oz) sugar
400ml (14fl oz) milk or buttermilk
2 eggs

Divide the butter into three equal knobs. Use 1 knob to grease the bottom and sides of a heavy frying pan and line the bottom with a circle of baking paper. Melt the rest of the butter in a separate saucepan without letting it get too hot. Break the eggs into a bowl and whisk in the milk and half the melted butter. Sift together the dry ingredients and stir into the egg mixture taking care not to over-mix. Pour into the frying pan and brush the top with the remaining butter. Cook on the top of the stove for about 20 minutes, turn and cook for a further 20 minutes. It is better cooked for about an hour in a moderate oven (180°C/350°F) as it tends to burn on the bottom unless you have a heat diffuser to put under the frying pan.

Wholemeal Bread   *Makes 2 large loaves*
This recipe was given to me by Rachael Hayward after she had spent Christmas cruising around Tierra del Fiego. Rachael recommends using stone-ground or wholemeal flour because, providing you can stop the crew gobbling the batch in one sitting, this type of bread will keep for at least a week.

2 900g (2lb) tins of stone-ground or wholemeal flour
1 level tablespoon dried yeast
1.2litres (2pts) water
1 teaspoon honey
1½ tablespoons salt
2 tablespoons oil

Heat the water to blood temperature and keep warm. Mix together the yeast and honey until creamy and then stir into half the warm water; leave until it is frothy. Mix the salt with the flour, tip into a large bowl and make a well in the centre.

When the yeast has proved, pour into the well and add the oil. Stir gradually drawing in the flour from the sides and carefully adding the rest of the warm water, but making sure that the dough does not get too sticky. Turn on to a floured surface and knead for 10–15 minutes. Dust the dough lightly with flour and put into a large plastic bag and leave in a warm place to rise until it has doubled in bulk. When the dough has risen, remove from the bag, punch down and divide between the two tins. Allow the dough to rise, which may be as long as an hour, depending on the ambient temperature.

Set oven to 190°C/37°F moderately hot. Bake for 20 minutes then look to see if the top is burning. If it is, lower the temperature and cook for a further 10–15 minutes. To test if the bread is cooked, remove a loaf from the tin and knock it on the bottom; it will sound hollow if it is cooked. Put on a rack to cool.

Banana Bread   *Makes 1 loaf*

110g (4oz) or 8 tablespoons butter
170g (6oz) or 12 tablespoons sugar
2 eggs
225g (8oz) flour
1 teaspoon baking powder
½ teaspoon salt
225g (8oz) wholewheat flour
3 large ripe bananas, mashed
1 teaspoon vanilla essence
110g (4oz) walnuts, chopped

In a large bowl cream together the butter and sugar until soft and fluffy. (This can be done in a food processor at home.) Add the eggs one at a time, beating well between. Sift together the flours, baking powder and salt and gradually beat into the mixture. Fold in the mashed bananas, walnuts and vanilla essence and pour into a greased bread tin. Preheat the oven to 180°C/350°F and bake the bread for about 1 hour or until a skewer inserted into the middle comes out clean. When cooked, remove from the oven and allow to cool for 10 minutes in the tin before turning out on to a wire rack.

CHAPTER FIFTEEN

Recipes – Fish and Shellfish

There is nothing to equal the taste of a mackerel that has come straight from the sea via a frying pan and on to your plate. The only snag is that either the fisherman don't catch enough for the whole crew, or you end up with more than you can eat in one sitting. It is a shame to throw them away, so either give the excess to someone else, or better still pickle them – they are just as delicious eaten cold. You can buy a do-it-yourself smoking kit, which is another attractive method of preserving fish and poultry as well. Small mackerel, or almost any really fresh fish, is delicious raw. Fillet in the normal way and then cover the fillets in lemon or lime juice. Leave for a few hours until the flesh has turned white. A little finely chopped chilli can be added if you like. To serve, drain off the liquid and add a little salt and freshly ground black pepper.

White Wine *Court Bouillon*

Fish poached in a white wine *court bouillon* will keep for a week in a fridge. It is best to make the real thing, but if it is not convenient, use a packet of fish *court bouillon* with a little extra wine added. There is no reason why this should not be made at home if you anticipate catching a lot of fish while cruising. It is not difficult to make on board, except that the rapid boiling required to reduce the liquid produces quite a lot of steam.

   1 bottle of dry white wine
   3 carrots, peeled and sliced
   4 onions, sliced
   bouquet garni
   12 black peppercorns
   1 stick celery, chopped

½ lemon, cut into thin slices
¼ teaspoon fennel seeds

Place all the ingredients into a deep saucepan, bring to the boil and reduce rapidly to half quantity. Leave to cool.

4 mackerel, less heads and tails, cleaned
1 teaspoon of pickling spice, including a red chilli

Place the mackerel in the bottom of a pan and strain the *court bouillon* over the top. Add the pickling spice and bring slowly to the boil. The moment the water is bubbling, count to three and then remove from the heat and allow to cool. Carefully remove the fish from the pan with a slotted spoon, lay them in a dish and carefully remove the skin and backbones. Reduce the *court bouillon* by half, cool, and then strain over the fish. Cover with tinfoil and put in a cool place until required. Mackerel or herring prepared this way will keep for up to a week in the fridge.

Gravad Lax is now seen on every menu, as it has been a fashionable way to serve salmon in this country in recent years. How the Scandinavians must laugh; they have been using this method of preserving raw salmon for aeons. Making Gravad Lax is not difficult and mackerel treated in a similar way is delicious; no one will guess what it is.

Marinated Mackerel (Gravad Lax style)   *Serves 6*
4 large fresh mackerel, less head, gutted and backbone removed
2 heaped tablespoons of salt
2 heaped tablespoons of brown sugar
2 teaspoons of crushed black peppercorns
2 tablespoons of fresh or dried dill weed
2 tablespoons gin

Split the fish and remove the backbone. Mix the dried ingredients together and moisten with the gin. Spread a little of the mixture over the bottom of a dish and lay the first fish skin-side down. Sprinkle with mixture and lay the next fish flesh-side down on top; repeat the same layers with the remaining fish leaving enough of the mixture to put on the remaining fish leaving enough of the mixture to put on the top. Cover tightly with tinfoil and use a similar dish or tin to weight the fish and press them together. Leave in a cool place for at least 12 hours, but no longer than 3 days.

To serve, remove the fish, drain and discard the liquid. Slice the flesh from the skin in much the same way as you would with smoked salmon. Make a dill-flavoured sauce by mixing a little mustard and dill with yoghurt or mayonnaise. Serve with fresh brown bread and an ice-cold glass of Dutch Genever gin.

Bobs Mackerel   *Serves 4–6*
A Belgian friend gave me this excellent recipe for preserving mackerel on board, when the fishermen have caught so many that you cannot think how to cook them next. Dutch gin is recommended, but any brand will do. Somehow gin offsets the oily flavour of mackerel to perfection; if you have any on board, the addition of a couple of crushed juniper berries is even better.

> 2 or more mackerel, filleted
> gin
> 55g (2oz) butter

Place the fillets flesh-side down in a deep pan and cover with gin. Cover the pan with a close-fitting lid and hide away in a cool place for at least 24 hours. (They will keep quite happily for at least three or more days depending on the weather.)

To cook the fish, drain and discard the liquid, then melt the butter in a frying pan. When it is foaming put in the fish, 2 fillets at a time and fry for about 3 minutes each side. Serve with brown bread and butter. Your guests will never guess that they are eating the humble mackerel.

Mackerel Baked in Foil   *Serves 4*
The smell of fried or grilled fish is not pleasant, as it tends to hang around the entire boat for ages, and many people find it nauseating. To minimize the offending odours, as well as producing a less rich-tasting dish, try cooking them this way baked in foil packets in the oven.

> 4 fresh mackerel
> 1 large onion, finely chopped
> fresh or dried rosemary

juice of 1 lemon
salt and pepper
55g (2oz) soft butter or margarine
4 individual squares of tinfoil

Remove the backbone, head, tail and fins. Wash in salt water and pat dry with kitchen paper. Lay each fish skin-side down on the buttered tinfoil squares and divide the onion and rosemary between them. Season with salt, pepper and the lemon juice. Fold one half of the fillet over and wrap up in the foil. Place the envelopes on a baking tray and bake in a preheated hot oven (220°C/425°F) for about 20–30 minutes depending on the size of the fish.

Brittany Chaudrée (from La Rochelle) *Serves 6*
  1.8kg (4lb) assorted fresh fish (but not mackerel) cleaned; if large, cut into chunks
  6 onions, peeled and quartered
  6 small-to-medium potatoes, scrubbed but not peeled, cut in half if very large
  3 cloves of garlic
  2 cloves
  large bouquet garni
  110g (4oz) butter
  salt and peppercorns
  1 litre (1¾pts) dry white wine

In a large, deep pot place the onions, potatoes, garlic, bouquet garni, peppercorns and sprinkle with about 1 teaspoon of salt. Arrange the cleaned fish on the top of the vegetables and cover with the wine. Add a little water if the wine does not cover the fish. Bring to the boil, cover and lower the heat and simmer gently for about 30 minutes. When the potatoes are cooked, remove them and the fish and keep on one side while you reduce the stock by about half. Check the seasoning, return the fish and potatoes to the pan and reheat for a minute, then serve with crusty bread and liberal quantities of white wine.

Mussel Chowder *Serves 6*
If you have a glut of mussels and have tried every other way of eating them, then this soup is an interesting variation on the traditional clam chowder.

1 large onion, chopped
55g (2oz) unsmoked streaky bacon, diced
3 large tomatoes, peeled or 1 small tin of tomatoes with as much of the
  juice squeezed out as possible
1 small sweet red pepper, or 1 small tin of pimentos, drained and chopped
1 small tin of sweetcorn
2 medium potatoes, cut into small cubes
1 bayleaf
16 litres (2¾pts) chicken stock, or water and stock cube
½ teaspoon curry powder
2 teaspoons arrowroot or cornflour
3 dozen mussels
a little nutmeg

Clean the mussels, steam open and reserve their juice. Put the bacon
in a saucepan and cook gently until the fat is beginning to run, add
the onion and cook until lightly browned. Add the potatoes, tomatoes,
peppers, sweetcorn, stock and curry powder. Simmer for about 25
minutes until the potatoes are soft. Mix the arrowroot or cornflour in
a cup with a little white wine or water and add to the stock, simmer
for a further 5 minutes. Add the mussels and their strained liquid
and heat through. Check the seasoning.

Stuffed Mussels   *Serves 4*
This is a rich and delicious dish that needs only a bottle or two or
dry white wine and fresh bread to be utterly memorable. A salad,
followed by a fresh peach or some grapes, is all you need to end the
meal.

1kg (2lb 3oz) mussels, or a bucketful
2 medium onions, finely chopped
3–4 cloves of garlic, finely chopped
parsley, finely chopped
2 slices of stale bread, crumbled
170–225g (6–8oz) soft butter (depending on the amount of mussels)

Wash and clean the mussels, discarding any that are broken or open.
Put the mussels in a large pan with a cup of fresh water and steam
until they are all open, about 5 minutes, shaking the pan from time
to time. Leave to cool while you prepare the stuffing. Mix together
the finely chopped onion, garlic, parsley and breadcrumbs. Season
with a little black pepper. When the mussels are cool enough to

handle, remove one half of the shell and place the other in one or more baking dishes. Put a teaspoon of the stuffing on top of each shell and place in a preheated hot oven (220°C/425°F) for about 10–15 minutes until they are sizzling and a golden brown.

Spaghetti and Cockles   *Serves 4*

This should be made with fresh cockles, but it is quite good made with tinned clams. On no account use cockles bought from a stall as they are likely to be soused in vinegar.

    225g (8oz) uncooked spaghetti
    1kg (2lb 3oz) cockles, cleaned
    170g (6oz) butter
    3–4 cloves of garlic, finely chopped
    parsley, finely chopped
    Parmesan cheese

Bring a large pan of water to the boil and add the spaghetti, return to the boil and cook for 12 minutes. Drain and keep warm. Steam the cockles open and remove from their shells. Melt the butter in a saucepan, add the garlic and cook gently for about three minutes. Raise the heat a little and add the cockles and parsley; stir once or twice then tip over the spaghetti and mix together. Serve in a large dish with Parmesan cheese and freshly ground black pepper.

Spaghetti with Clam Sauce   *Serves 4*

This is delicious made with tinned clams and the mixed juices with the addition of vodka is an excellent drink.

    1 425g (15oz) tin clams in their own juice, drained
    1 425g (15oz) tin peeled tomatoes, drained
    1 teaspoon dried oregano
    2 tablespoons freshly chopped parsley
    1 teaspoon capers
    ½ teaspoon sugar
    1 teaspoon salt
    225g (8oz) uncooked spaghetti

Drain the tin of tomatoes and squeeze as much of the juice out of them as possible. Put the tomatoes into a small saucepan and crush them with a fork. Add the capers, sugar, oregano and parsley, bring to the boil and cook until the sauce has reduced to a fairly thick consistency. Bring a large pan of salted water to the boil and add the spaghetti, return to boiling point, cover and cook for 12 minutes. Drain and keep warm. Add the drained clams to the tomato sauce and reheat for a minute or two without letting the sauce boil. Check the seasoning, add a little lemon juice if necessary; pour over and mix with the spaghetti.

Moules à la Marinière   *Serves 6–8*

This can be either the most delectable dish of all time if well cooked, or a nightmare of rubbery mussels awash in a pale liquid full of salt and grit. Most people have their own variations; here is my favourite.

  1 bucket of scrubbed and cleaned mussels
  2 large onions, sliced
  2 cloves of garlic, chopped
  30g (1oz) butter
  2 glasses of dry white wine
  1 bayleaf
  2 tablespoons freshly chopped parsley
  150ml (¼pt) cream

Melt the butter in a deep saucepan over a gentle heat, add the onion and garlic and cook until the onion is transparent. Add the mussels, bayleaf and wine, cover with a lid and cook over a high heat for about 6 minutes, shaking the pan from time to time until all the mussels are opened. Remove the mussels and onion with the aid of a slotted spoon into a separate dish and keep warm. Taste the mussel liquor, if it is very salty, strain about half into a clean saucepan, or if not, reduce until you are left with about half a pint. Stir in the cream, check the seasoning, pour over the mussels, sprinkle with parsley and serve at once.

Devilled Crab   *Serves 4–6*

This is simple to prepare once you have cooked the crab and picked all the flesh out of the shell.

  1 medium-to-large crab or 2–3 smaller ones
  ½ green pepper, finely chopped
  1 onion, finely chopped
  ½ teaspoon dried mustard

pinch of cayenne pepper
110g (4oz) breadcrumbs
110g (4oz) melted butter
1 egg yolk
finely chopped parsley
lemon juice

Mix the crab meat with all the ingredients, but keeping half the breadcrumbs on one side. Taste and add a little salt and pepper if required. Pack the mixture into the scrubbed shell and sprinkle the remaining breadcrumbs on the top. Dot with butter and put in a moderately hot oven until lightly browned.

Sardines

The finest sardines I have eaten were in Camaret at one of the quayside restaurants. Our noses led us to this particular one as the smell of grilling sardines was irresistible. They were brought to the table straight from the charcoal grill where they had been grilled with fresh herbs. I discovered the grill later in the evening *en route* for the only loo, out at the back.

To cook them yourself, wash and sprinkle with herbs and grill both sides until brown. Do not attempt to fry them as they fall to pieces.

Herring and Oatmeal   *Serves 4*

The oatmeal is a good contrast to the oil flesh of herring and is a traditional way of cooking them in the Orkney Islands.

4 cleaned herring
55g (2oz) medium-cut oatmeal
55g (2oz) butter cut into slivers
salt and pepper

Split the herring and remove the backbone but leave the roe, if any, in place. Lay them open, skin side down and press the oatmeal firmly into the flesh, sprinkle with salt and pepper and dot with the butter. Grill for about 5 minutes.

Cullen Skink   *Serves 4*

This is the classic recipe from *The Scottish Cookery Book*, by Elizabeth Craig. According to Alan Davidson, in his fascinating book *North*

Atlantic Seafood, haddock do not take to salting as well as cod. The traditional methods of curing were therefore drying and smoking. 'Rizzared' haddock in Scotland were sun-dried; those dried on the rocks at Collieston were known as Collieston speldings and could be eaten raw. 'Hazel haddocks' were the small ones that were simply hung to dry in the rigging of fishing boats and were the perks of the apprentices. The most famous of all were those produced by the fishing village of Finnan, near Aberdeen, where haddock were smoked over a peat-reek and sold as Finnan haddocks. Peat is no longer used, and large quantities are smoked elsewhere, but Finnan haddock have maintained their reputation.

1 medium-sized Finnan haddock
1 onion, finely chopped
500ml (1pt) milk
15g (½oz) butter
Mashed potatoes
1 tablespoon finely chopped parsley
salt and pepper

Skin the haddock and put it with the onion in a shallow pan with enough water to cover. Bring slowly to the boil and simmer for about 10 minutes. Remove the fish and flake the flesh away from the bones. Return the bones to the pan of water, cover and continue to simmer for ½-¾ hour. Strain the stock into a clean pan, add the milk and bring to the boil, simmer for 5 minutes then add the flaked fish and enough mashed potato to make a creamy soup. Just before serving, stir in the butter and parsley.

CHAPTER SIXTEEN

Recipes – The Main Course

Chicken with a Crusty Topping   *Serves 4*
This is a quick and easy way of reviving the remains of yesterday's
roast. It is also delicious enough to persuade everyone that you have
spent hours slaving over a hot stove.

    1 small cooked chicken
    2 medium leeks, cleaned and sliced
    1 150g (6oz) tin sweetcorn, drained
    1 225g (8oz) tin condensed mushroom soup
    2 tablespoons cream, or milk
    1 tablespoon fresh tarragon, chopped, or 1 teaspoon dried tarragon
    3 slices of brown bread, cut into cubes
    85g (3oz) butter
    1 tablespoon oil
    2 tablespoons Parmesan cheese

Remove the skin and flesh from the chicken and cut into bite-sized
chunks. Set the oven to 200°C, moderately hot. Melt 1oz of the butter
in a saucepan over a moderate heat, add the chopped leeks and cook
for a few minutes until soft. Spread the leeks in the bottom of an
oven-proof dish. Mix together the sweetcorn and the mushroom soup
with the cream or milk. Add the tarragon and diced chicken, then
spread on top of the leeks. Cover with the cubes of brown bread. Cut
the remaining butter into small pieces and scatter over the top of the
bread, drizzle with the tablespoon of oil and finally dust with Parmesan
cheese. Put in the oven for about 20–30 minutes until the top is crusty
brown and the mixture bubbling hot. Serve with plain noodles or rice
and a salad.

Barbecued Spare-rib Sauce   *Serves 4*

Spare ribs are tasty and a favourite dish with most people. They must be cooked long enough for the meat almost to drop off the bone. The first part of the cooking can be done at home and the final preheat and crisping on board, either under the grill or in the oven. The sauce in which they are pre-cooked can be frozen and re-used.

> 900g (2lb) pork spare ribs, divided into individual ribs
> oil for browning (optional)
> *Sauce:*
> 900ml (1½ pts) chicken stock
> 2 teaspoons chilli powder or tabasco sauce
> 2 teaspoons sugar
> juice of two oranges
> 2 tablespoons soy sauce
> 1 tablespoon yellow bean paste
> 2 tablespoons Hoisin sauce
> 3 cloves of garlic, finely chopped
> 4 spring onions, finely chopped
> a slice of fresh ginger, about the size of a 2 pence piece peeled and chopped.

Either heat the oil in a large frying pan and fry the ribs until golden brown, or heat a heavy-bottomed pan and dry fry the ribs without oil. To prevent the meat from sticking the pan must be very hot. Whichever method you use, when the ribs are brown, drain them on kitchen paper.

Combine all the ingredients for the sauce in a deep casserole and bring to the boil. Add the ribs and simmer for 1 hour until the meat is tender when tested with a fork. Remove the ribs and put on one side. Taste the sauce: it should be reduced by about half and quite strong in flavour; if not, it may require further reducing. Leave the sauce to cool and when quite cold skim the fat from the surface. When ready to eat the ribs, pre-heat the oven or grill to moderately hot (200°C/400°F) and lay the ribs on a baking tray and bake or grill for about 15 minutes until brown, basting from time to time with the sauce.

Hamburgers   *Serves 4*

Ready-made hamburgers will last reasonably well providing they are kept in a cool place. I sometimes add a little minced onion to the mixture, but only if I know they will be eaten straightaway.

550g (1lb 4oz) lean minced beef
55g (2oz) smoked bacon, minced
1 tablespoon parsley, finely chopped
4 pinches of chilli powder
salt and pepper
oil

In a large bowl combine the beef, bacon, chilli powder and salt and mix thoroughly together. Divide the mixture into four and pat into hamburger shapes. Brush each hamburger with a little oil and grill under a very hot grill 2 minutes each side. Serve in a bun with relish, onion rings, lettuce and tomatoes. To store frozen or fresh, wrap each hamburger in cling film.

Fish Cakes   *Serves 4*

These are equally good hot or cold as a main course or a light first course. A garlicky mayonnaise or spicy tomato sauce is a good accompaniment.

450g (1lb) cod or haddock, fresh or frozen, skinned
110g (4oz) fresh breadcrumbs
4 pinches of chilli powder
1 tablespoon parsley, finely chopped
1 small piece of grated fresh ginger
1 egg
1 egg yolk
1 tablespoon flour
a knob of butter and oil for frying

It is much easier to skin frozen fillets of fish before they thaw. Having skinned the fish, mince or chop in a food processor. In a large bowl combine the minced fish with the spring onions, parsley, chilli and grated ginger and mix together thoroughly with your hands. Break the egg into a small bowl, add the yolk and beat thoroughly with a fork, then tip into the fish and mix together using a fork or wooden spoon. With very well-floured hands divide the fish into about 12 pieces and roll into balls roughly the same size as a golf ball and flatten them slightly with the palm of your hand.

Heat in a large frying pan a tablespoon of oil and a knob of butter until sizzling, then slide the fish cakes carefully into the pan and immediately baste the top with a spoon of hot oil. Fry gently for two minutes on each side. Remove with a slotted spoon and drain on kitchen paper. Eat warm or cold.

Salmon spaghetti   *Serves 4*

To be really authentic this recipe should be made with a mixture of fresh and smoked salmon. If fresh salmon is not available, replace it with tinned. There is no substitute for smoked salmon but, as you can buy it vacuum-packed, there is no reason why a couple of packets of salmon scraps should not be included in the stores list. The off-cuts of a side of smoked salmon are often sold as scraps and are more economical than the genuine article.

> 450g (1lb) spaghetti
> 25g (1oz) butter
> 1 bunch of spring onions, finely chopped
> 275ml (10fl oz) single cream or strained yoghurt
> 1 teaspoon fresh dill *or* ½ teaspoon dried dill
> 2 tablespoons white wine
> 225g (8oz) cooked fresh salmon, skinned and boned
> 170g (6oz) smoked salmon scraps, sliced into neat slivers

Bring a large saucepan of water to boil with a little salt. When the water is bubbling, tip in the spaghetti, bring back to the boil, stir and then cover the saucepan with a tea-cloth and put the lid on. Turn off the heat and leave for 12 minutes. Drain and rinse under hot water.

Melt the butter in a saucepan and when hot add the chopped spring onions and cook over a moderate heat for about 5 minutes until the onions are soft. Stir in the cream or yoghurt, wine and dill and simmer for a minute or two. Pour over the spaghetti, add the two salmons and reheat gently, then serve immediately.

Rat Soufflé   *Serves 4*

The making of a good soufflé is sometimes considered to be almost as black an art as astronavigation. Like all myths, it has been exaggerated out of all proportion so that everyone thinks how clever you are. Choose your moment carefully if you make this on board as falling off the top of the wave at the wrong moment will guarantee that the crew's hopes will fall as flat as the soufflé.

> 55g (2oz) butter
> 45g (1½oz) plain flour

300ml (½pt) milk
1 400g (14oz) tin of *ratatouille*
1 dessertspoon of fresh basil, chopped (if available)
4 eggs, separated

Make a roux by melting the butter in a small saucepan and adding the flour, stirring well. When mixed, withdraw the pan from the heat and gradually beat in the milk until smooth and thick. Return to the heat and cook gently for about 10 minutes. Season to taste. Add the tin of *ratatouille* and mix thoroughly, crushing some of the larger lumps of aubergine so that they are not too large. Beat in the egg yolks. When the mixture is cool, beat the egg whites until dry and stiff and fold into the mixture. Turn into a buttered soufflé dish and cook in a moderately hot oven until risen and brown on the top, about 30 minutes.

Kedgeree   *Serves 4*

Whatever rice-based meal I cook, I always use Basmati rice. It is easy to cook and has a wonderful taste and smell. This version uses raw smoked haddock and is wonderful either hot or cold as a salad. Kedgeree is just as good made with tinned salmon.

2 cups of uncooked rice
2 cups of water
450g (1lb) smoked haddock
4 hard-boiled eggs, roughly chopped
55g (4oz) butter
bunch of parsley, finely chopped
black pepper

Put the rice in a sieve and run under the fresh-water tap until the water is clear. Put the rice in a heavy-bottomed saucepan with two cups of fresh water. Bring the rice to the boil uncovered, stirring a couple of times. When the water has almost evaporated and the top of the rice is pock-marked with small holes, turn off the heat, cover the pan with a tea-towel and put on the lid. Leave for 12 minutes. Cut the raw smoked haddock into strips, carefully removing any bones. When the rice is ready, add the strips of fish and the butter and stir together to mix. Replace the lid and put on a very low heat for about 5 minutes, checking to see that it is not burning on the bottom. At the last moment, add the hard-boiled eggs and parsley, season and serve at once.

A final note on cooking rice. One breakfast cup of uncooked rice will serve two people. Whatever size of measure you use for the rice, use the same for the water: 1 cup of rice to 1 cup of water. The rice must be prewashed until the water runs clear, and for this you can use salt water first and then a final rinse with fresh. Never add salt to the cooking water, and always bring to the boil until almost all the water has evaporated; cover tightly so that you never let any of the precious steam escape.

Racy Italian Pasta   *Serves 4*
This is a very quick and cheap sauce to make.

> 450g (1lb) pasta
> 2 teaspoons of salt
> 2 1kg (2lbs 3oz) tins of tomatoes, drained
> 4 tablespoons olive oil
> 1 teaspoon dried oregano
> 110g (4oz) black olives
> 55g (2oz) capers, drained and chopped
> 4 cloves of garlic, chopped
> 1 small tin of anchovy fillets, drained and chopped
> 3 tablespoons chopped parsley
> freshly ground black pepper

Bring a large saucepan of water to the boil, add the salt and the pasta, return to the boil, stir and simmer for 12 minutes, drain and keep the pasta warm. Drain the tomatoes and squeeze as much juice out of each tomato as possible; reserve the juice to drink with vodka while you are cooking. Put the tomatoes into a saucepan with the olive oil and break them up with a fork. Bring to the boil and add the rest of the ingredients, stirring continually until the sauce has reduced and is thick enough for your liking. Divide the pasta into four bowls, pour over the sauce and eat at once with a spoonful of Parmesan cheese. Wash down with quantities of a full-bodied red wine.

'Rose Rambler' Stew   *Serves 2*
Finally, if the crew complain about the standard of your cooking, offer the one who complains the loudest this as an alternative. This was given to me by the wife of the late Hum Barton, a highly distinguished

yachtsman. Mary emphasizes that this is Hum's recipe and that she had nothing to do with it.

2lb rotten beef
¼lb mouldy bacon
1 bad egg
1 small piece of driftwood, chopped small
2 feet of old rope, well shredded
12 cigarette stubs
2 tablespoons of diesel oil
¼pt bilge water

Wipe meat on engine. Heat cooker until red hot; add diesel oil and cook meat until black. Add bilge water and all other ingredients, cover. Place on high heat and when steam escapes place weight on vent pipe. If steam does not escape take no notice. Cook for 24 hours. Remove from heat and have another drink while cooker cools. Garnish with varnish and serve lukewarm.

If cooker explodes, buy another yacht and try again, but reduce diesel oil by one-third.

CHAPTER SEVENTEEN

Recipes – Sweet Dreams, A Few Puddings

One summer in Turkey, our youngest daughter suddenly asked me if I could make a Black Forest gâteau. 'Yes', I replied. 'Now?' she asked hopefully. With the temperature soaring into the 100s, it was the last thing I had any intention of thinking about, let alone making. However, one of Vanessa's ardent admirers rowed across the bay to Gocek and reappeared with a Turkish version. The cake was coated in a thick chocolate icing and decorated with sickly Dayglo green squiggles. Vanessa was in seventh heaven. I have since discovered a chocolate sauce which is a quick substitute when there is no Black Forest gâteau to be had for love or money.

Best-ever Chocolate Sauce   *Serves 4–6*
This is simple to make on board or at home and the joy is that it keeps for a week or two in the fridge – providing it is kept well hidden. It can be used hot or cold, poured over ice cream or profiteroles.

  100g (3½oz) dark chocolate
  150ml (¼ pt) double cream

Break the chocolate into squares and place with the cream in a heat-proof bowl over a saucepan of hot water. Bring the water to simmering point, stirring the mixture continually until the chocolate has melted. Remove from the heat and cool until thick. Poor into a jar and keep in the fridge until required.

Mars Sauce   *Serves 4*
This is also wonderful over ice-cream or tinned pears.

2 Mars bars
1 tablespoon strong black coffee
1 tablespoon rum

Cut the Mars bars into cubes and put in a saucepan with the coffee and rum. Melt very slowly, stirring from time to time.

Chestnut Cream
Serves 4–6

1 400g (14oz) tin of sweet chestnut purée
300ml (½pt) whipping cream (long-life cream will do)
juice of ½ a lemon

Stir a spoonful of cream into the chestnut purée to thin down. Whisk the cream until it is standing in peaks and fold into the chestnut purée. Stir in a little of the lemon juice; if it is still too sweet, add a little more lemon.

Trifle
Serves 6

Trifle has always been a favourite family pudding when sailing, although it never seems to be quite so popular on shore.

1 stale sponge cake
sweet sherry and brandy (3:1 sherry to brandy)
home-made strawberry or raspberry jam
600ml (1pt) custard
4–6 ratafia biscuits
150ml (¼pt) whipping cream
almonds, blanched and split

Cut the cake in fingers and arrange in the bottom of a suitable dish or plastic box. Pour over the sherry and brandy and allow the cake to soak up the liquid. Spread the jam. Crush the ratafia biscuits and scatter over the cake. Make the custard and while still warm, pour over the cake and biscuits. (If using tinned custard, warm it first in a saucepan.) When the custard is quite cold, whip the cream and pile on top. Decorate with the almonds.

Gingerbread
Serves 6

'Had I but one penny in the world, thou shoudst have it for gingerbread'
(*Love's Labour's Lost*)

Gingerbread keeps for ages providing it is not sliced and is well wrapped in waxed paper and foil. Simply wonderful on its own or eaten with a slice of good farmhouse Cheddar.

> 340g (12oz) flour
> 1 heaped teaspoon baking powder
> 1½ teaspoons ground ginger
> ½ teaspoon salt
> 110g (4oz) sugar
> 1 egg, beaten
> 8 tablespoons molasses
> 4 tablespoons boiling water
> 4 tablespoons light cooking oil (not olive)

Pre-set oven to 180°C/350°F (moderate). Sift together the flour, baking powder and ginger into a bowl. Stir in the sugar and salt. Add the lightly beaten egg and the molasses and mix together thoroughly. Add the boiling water and oil and beat until smooth. Grease and flour a square baking pan, pour in the mixture and cook for about 30–40 minutes until the top springs back when lightly pressed. Cool and cut into fingers.

Dried Fruit   *Serves 4*

The addition of rum makes this quite a treat; vodka can be used instead.

> 450g (1lb) mixed dried fruit
> 600ml (1pt) water
> 1 glass of rum

Soak the fruit in the water until it has plumped out. Cook gently until the fruit is soft and the water almost evaporated, add the rum and simmer for about 5 more minutes. Serve with whipped cream or custard.

CHAPTER EIGHTEEN

Spares

When I began thinking about the contents of this book I did not imagine it including a list of spares as well. Then I realized that spares are just as vital as provisions for, unless you can repair a broken part, you may well be at sea for so much longer and consequently you may run out of food. It is pointless jamming a bag of eclectic hardware into a cubby-hole and hoping that somewhere inside it is the spare mainsail shackle or pump valve. Like everything else, spares deserve detailed planning.

The length and type of voyage planned will dictate the type of spare parts you will need to take. An ex-Admiral's-Cup racer told me quite seriously that they never took any spares not required by the rules. If anything broke they simply turned on the engine and motored home, with the race given up as lost. This attitude may apply to that kind of racing, but even in Channel Handicap races, and definitely in long-distance ocean racing, spares are essential. Long-distance cruising yachtsmen have to take into consideration that some spare parts may be difficult to obtain or at least more expensive far away from home and therefore must plan accordingly. You cannot possibly take a full inventory of spares otherwise you would have to tow a spare boat.

Having made your basic list then consider what additional items you may need for a longer voyage.

RIGGING – STANDING AND RUNNING

It would be quite impossible to take a spare set of everything, but you do want to have the wherewithal to be able to improvize in case of a major rigging failure such as dismasting or losing a shroud. What you need will depend largely on your type of boat and knowing her little foibles. Desmond knew from experience that *Gipsy Moth V*'s backstay had tremendous stresses on it, so when it parted in the South Atlantic in the middle of the night despite having been renewed only three months previously, he was prepared for this and was able to replace the broken one. Here are some suggestions:

Blocks – Snatch blocks, blocks with beckets, single and double
D-clamps – A substitute for splicing wire rigging
Halyard – If all your halyards are led internally through the mast it is a good precaution to have a light messenger rove as an external halyard that could double for the jib or main. For long-distance sailing, I would carry an extra made-up halyard as well
Pelican hook
Rigging screws – Sometimes called bottle-screws or turnbuckles
Shackles – Assorted sizes and shapes, including link and snap shackles
Sheets – One pair, long enough to replace spinnaker sheets if necessary
Spinnaker fittings – If you carry two spinnaker poles these can be used to make a jury rig if you lose the mast. Spare cup fittings on slides that fit the Genoa track to hold the bottom of the poles in place saves ruining stanchions.
Split pins – In many different sizes
Strops – Wire strops with thimbles and wire rope grips (D clamps) can be used should you need to mend a stay or shroud
Thimbles – Plastic and stainless steel

SAILS

Battens – Instead of taking a spare set, take a couple of lengths which you can then cut to size
Needles – Assorted sizes. Coated in Vaseline and wrapped in cling film or stuck into a wedge of polystyrene keeps them from rusting
Palm – Essential. Left-handed crew members should bring their own
Patches – Overlapping Genoas suffer badly from chafe where they come in contact with the pulpit and the crosstrees. Get your friendly sailmaker to cut you several patches for the vulnerable areas
PVC tape – For electrical repairs and anti-chafe

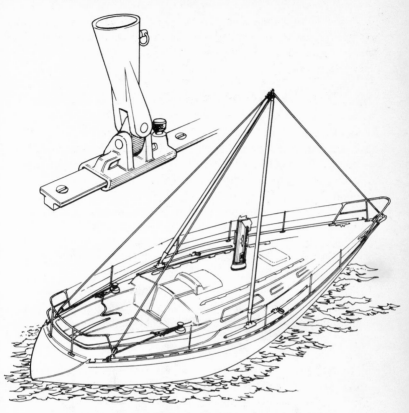

17.   Using spinnaker pole fittings for jury rig

Slides – Spare mainsail slides
Spinnaker tape – Very useful for quick repairs
Tape – Double sided, to stick down patches in the correct place
   prior to sewing them down
Tape – 7m (23ft) of 25mm-(1in) wide webbing tape. It is cheap,
   pliable and strong and can be used in many applications – such
   as replacing slides that have come off the mainsail
Duck tape – For repairs, anti-chafe and most things in between
Twine – For stitching and whipping

ELECTRICS

Batteries – For torches and all battery-operated instruments
Battery-state tester – For checking 1.5v batteries
Bulbs – Masthead, cabin and compass
Fuses – You can't have enough. Make sure you carry the right size for all the electrics – radios, SatNav, Decca, etc. – as well as for the domestic lighting
Hygrometer – For checking battery electrolyte, unless you have sealed batteries
Insulating tape – Electrical connections
Extension leads – Clip on
Junction box – Small junction boxes that look like a bar of chocolate
Light switches – Spare toggle switches for any snapped off
Multi-purpose meter – For testing electrical circuits
Torch – The best waterproof torch I have ever come across is made by Pifco who also make small pocket torches. Very handy on deck at night; each crew member ideally should have his or her own.

ENGINE

Even on a small yacht two batteries are essential. They should be fitted with an isolating switch so that one is for domestic use and the other for starting the engine. (If your engine can be started by hand, see that everyone knows how.) The one thing that is vital as far as engine maintenance goes is knowing how to bleed the system.

Engine anodes – If your engine has them
Engine oil
Filters
Gaskets
Impeller
Injectors
Jubilee clips of assorted sizes
Rubber hose
Stern gland grease

MISCELLANEOUS

Baggywrinkle – Invaluable anti-chafe

Foam spray – Sold by builder's merchants for insulation and the fitting of windows, this epoxy foam comes as an aerosol spray which expands on exposure to the air and sets hard. It is the best way I know of curing drips from badly seated Genoa tracks or winch pads; it needs a wet surface for it to 'go off'. It looks rather like the inside of a Crunchie bar

Fog horn – Spare aerosol cylinders

Glass fibre – A large piece of matting and a two-part glass fibre repair kit that works even under water – in case you should get holed beneath the water line

Lines – Spare reef lines, and if you have an Aries self-steering gear, tiller lines

Mask and snorkel – For inspecting hull and propeller

Marline spike – Or a spare shackle key

Nuts and bolts

Plastic tubing – Assorted lengths and widths

Pump spares – For the loo and bilge pumps

Rag bag – Ours consists of assorted old shirts and pants. Useful for 101 odd things from padding to mopping-up spilt diesel

Silicon compound – Useful for all kinds of seals and joins

Silicon spray – Good for luff grooves and mainsail slides

Washers

WD 40 – Where should we be without it?

Winch parts – The manufacturer of your winches will be able to supply you with a handy collection of pawls, springs, ringclips and spacers quite cheaply

Wood – Even if your boat is fibreglass through and through, odd lengths of wood come in handy for many jobs from being used as a chopping or drilling block to being used to wedge or shore up displaced or damaged areas

TOOLS

Most engines are supplied with a small specialized tool kit. In addition to this the following list would make a good working tool bag:

Adjustable spanner
Allen keys – Have the habit of disappearing quite mysteriously
  when needed to take a winch apart. Also used on Aries self-
  steering gear and apt to be dropped overboard at the moment
  critique
Bits – Spares for the drill
Bolt croppers – Or a sharp heavy-duty hacksaw for cutting away
  rigging
Bolts
Electrical wire-strippers
Hacksaw blades
Hacksaw – And spare blades
Hammer
Hand drill and bits
Mallet
Mole wrench
Nuts, bolts and screws of various sizes
Philips screwdriver (star headed)
Pliers
Pop riveter
Screwdrivers – Three different sizes
Snipe-nosed pliers
Socket kit
Soldering-iron (12v)
Stilson wrench

Finally, a box with divided compartments, usually sold in stores like
Woolworths, is ideal for all the small things like bolts, nuts and split
pins. Old jam jars or yoghurt cartons can also be used to keep the
spares and tool locker organized. Libby Purves tells me that she and
her husband, Paul Heiney, keep their spare nuts and bolts in plastic
sweet jars, preferably the ones which still have 'Imperial mints', or
'Lollipops' on the labels as they are a convenient shape and size to
stow in the bilges. It is an excellent idea and, apart from that, I rather
like the idea of asking someone to pass you a number two humbug
when you are upside down grovelling in among the engine's intestines.

CHAPTER NINETEEN

Laying-up and De-storing

The marina berth has many advantages, mains electricity and easy access being the most obvious. This, and the advent of marine central heating systems, means that being in commission all year round is easily possible and some think negates the necessity of laying-up at all. One very good reason for not laying-up is that there are plenty of lovely winter weekends to enjoy in anchorages that are overcrowded during the summer. I'm a year-round sailing advocate. So, increasingly, are others. The yacht still has to come out of the water at some time for routine hull and skin-fitting inspection as well as antifouling. Standing and running rigging still need checking over, so what might be the winter laying-up instead becomes the autumn clean and clear-up, with a spring haul-out for antifouling and underwater examinations.

Scrub-out – At the end of the season, whenever it is, it really is worth all the hard work involved to remove all gear and stores from your boat and scrub through the whole of the inside with fresh water. Any areas that have become black with mould should be scrubbed off with a solution of bleach or Milton, then a fungus preventive should be applied, which may help to stop it growing all over again – hard work but worth it. Empty your water tanks – there is nothing so vile as water that has absorbed the taste of fibreglass tanks. Andrew Bray told me that when he had just joined the staff of *Yachting Monthly* he was taken by the redoubtable editor, Des Sleightholme, to help him fit out his boat at the beginning of the season. It was long, cold work and when at last a cup of tea was offered, Andrew accepted it like a man emerging from a Siberian salt mine. He nearly choked at the first sip, but 'new boy' as he was and in awe of the great man, did not dare say anything or even chuck the lethal mixture overboard.

Somehow he swallowed it down; no sooner had he finished it than Des picked up his mug, took a sip and spat it out in disgust saying, 'Ugh – filthy water. I can't think how you managed to drink it.'

Sheets and warps can be taken home and put into the washing machine quite safely as long as they don't have shackles or spinnaker fittings attached; use cold wash, as I don't want people telling me that all their sheets have shrunk or got rock hard in the wash. Small sails can be hosed down with fresh water and then hung on a washing line to drip dry.

Sails are expensive and should be cared for in the same way that you treat your best suit. For example, would you wash your best suit, wring it out, tumble-dry it and still expect it to fit? Of course not. But how many people do you see in marinas all round the country washing off their spinnakers and then hanging them up to let them flap themselves to death? Their owners are under the impression that this is the way to dry their sails, when all it is doing is ruining the sail. They may well be the same sort of people who you see motoring at full speed, head to wind, with their mainsail up and flogging the leach and battens to death. How much better for boat and sail it would be if instead they motored with their mainsail filled on one tack or the other. Large sails that are badly stained should be sent to a sailmaker that offers a valet service. Modern sailcloth is sturdy and more harm is done to the sail by leaving it stuffed anyhow into a bag or locker than by not washing out the salt. So make sure that all your sails are left neatly folded.

LEAKS

Modern hulls tend to leak less than old wooden boats, but few yachts are bone dry. There are at least five main sources of water getting into a boat; through deck fittings such as shroud plates, Genoa tracks or winch plates: from the stern glands; badly seated hatches; round the deck aperture of a keel-stepped mast; and through the heads. You may not even notice water getting in during your first season, if you are lucky not to have many arduous passages.

The first signs of damp may be noticed in a clothes locker, where the most likely source will be chain plates or Genoa track. To tackle this problem will involve taking down the overhead linings, which is a tedious occupation if they are not in sections. However, once these are removed you should be able to see where the water is getting in. Winch pads may need to be reseated, a job which is not too difficult to do yourself. Water coming in through the chain plates may indicate that you have a fairly serious problem. Unless you know what you are doing, it is the sort of job for a yard to tackle. Genoa tracks are notorious for leaks. The only permanent cure is to rebed the track. Drips down the mast are a nightmare. First of all there is the problem of getting all the chocks well seated so they don't fall out. Second, a decent 'gaiter' round the mast securely fixed with jubilee clips with the whole lot gunked up with silicon rubber will usually solve the problem. Condensation from the mast and tie rods is unavoidable unless they are covered with foam-lined vinyl. Yachts that have shallow bilges are a nightmare, as a couple of cups of water in the bottom, not noticed when you are upright, will reach places that you would not believe possible when well heeled.

The totally-stripped-out yacht may not be very beautiful, but there are some practical advantages. Without the paraphernalia of furniture and headlinings, it is much easier to trace the source if the water is getting in somewhere. Likewise, the electric cables that run in conduits are more accessible if you do not have to dismantle half the inside of your boat.

VENTILATION

Ventilation, or the lack of it, is the precursor of mould and a nasty smell the permeates boats which have been shut up for too long. Black stains appear on headlinings especially around the galley where grease has splashed, in the heads, and any place that regularly gets splashed with salt water.

Prevention is easier than cure. First of all, air must be able to circulate through the boat even when all the hatches are shut. Air will circulate if there is a ventilation point in the bows and another well aft; a wash board with its own louvre is the obvious solution there. If cruising in a hot climate, a miniature oscillating fan mounted on a bulkhead is certainly worth while. A Ventaxia in the heads is also a good idea.

When leaving your boat for more than a week at a time, leave locker doors open to allow air to circulate round the contents. It is essential

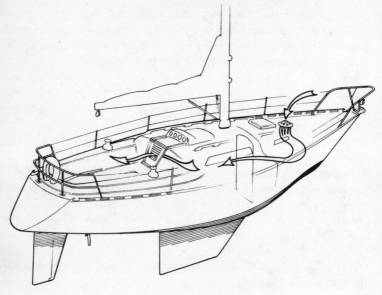

18. Flow of ventilation

to make sure when you leave your boat that she is clean and that if you have had a wet passage that everything inside and out has been washed down with fresh water. To stop clothes either getting damp or smelly, I recommend vacuum-sealing them in polythene bags. Damp clothes are more than a nuisance: they are a misery. To get over this problem I found an ingenious gadget that proved to be the answer to my prayers: a small vacuum packer normally used for deep-freezing food in polythene bags. Not only did it prove to be a boon for knickers and socks, but I have also used it most successfully for packing loaves of bread, cake and other goods that I wanted to keep dry. Black & Decker make a battery-operated vacuum cleaner designed for cleaning car upholstery, which is equally good for boats.

UPHOLSTERY AND CUSHIONS

When the first fabric upholstery appeared, I have to confess that I was among the cynics who thought that it would never replace the tough and practical vinyl-covered saloon seats. It was felt that the fabric would soon look tired and stained after a season or two of being soaked with salt water and suffering from the effects of having tomato ketchup and coffee ground into it by a clumsy crew. I still have my doubts about the wisdom of pastel blue dralon, but textured and tweedy types of material are certainly hard wearing and remain looking good for years, as any number of charter boat owners will testify. Besides which, it is far nicer to sit and sleep on than vinyl which can feel cold, or sticky in hot weather.

CONCLUSION

The sad sight of an unloved yacht parked in a marina or swinging on a mooring, her topsides filthy, warps green with mould and the tattered remains of a flag flapping from the crosstrees, makes me speculate as to why she has all the symptoms of being abandoned. For many people, once they have purchased their house and car, their next most significant expenditure will be on a yacht; their morale must have been at a low ebb to allow her to fall into this state. Maybe her owners bought her with the idea of family cruising, only to discover after the first flush of enthusiasm that their dream foundered on the cold hard bones of reality. Perhaps their plans were too ambitious or maybe they were unprepared.

Preparation is essential for the successful execution of any undertaking, whatever the scale. The crew with the highest morale do not necessarily step off that powerful-looking cruiser or the sleek racing machine; more likely they sail aboard a modest kind of craft. Morale cannot be measured by achievement alone. Morale is about the crew's confidence not only in the boat and skipper but also in their own abilities. Their spirits will be high because at the end of the day enormous satisfaction has been derived from having achieved what they set out to accomplish.

I hope that this book will help people with the planning stages so when they set off on their cruise not only will the boat be prepared to cope with most eventualities but that the demands of the inner man will be well catered for as well.

Weights and Measures

WEIGHTS		LIQUID MEASURES	
1 teaspoon = 1 level teaspoon			
1 tablespoon = 1 level tablespoon			
15g	½oz	10ml	1cl
20g	¾oz	75cl	1bottle
30g	1oz	120ml	4fl oz
55g	2oz	150ml	¼pt
85g	3oz	175ml	6fl oz
100g	3½oz	200ml	⅓pt
110g	4oz	250ml	8fl oz
140g	5oz	300ml	½pt
170g	6oz	350ml	12fl oz
200g	7oz	400ml	14fl oz
225g	8oz	450ml	¾pt
255g	9oz	500ml	18fl oz
285g	10oz	600ml	1pt
310g	11oz	750ml	1¼pts
340g	12oz	900ml	1½pts
370g	13oz	1litre	1¾pts
400g	14oz	1.2litres	2pts
425g	15oz	1.25litres	2¼pts
450g	1lb	1.5litres	2½pts
500g	1lb 2oz	1.6litres	2¾pts
570g	1lb 4oz	1.75litres	3pts
680g	1lb 8oz	2litres	3½pts
900g	2lb		
1kg	2lb 3oz		

Handy measures   Although grammes and ounces have been speci-fied in the recipes, few poeple keep kitchen scales on board, so here are some handy measures which, allied to your own judgement, will help you guess the weights more accurately.

3 teaspoons = 1 tablespoon
16 tablespoons = 1 cup
1 cup = ½pint

		approximately
breadcrumbs, fresh	30g (1oz)	7 level tablespoons
butter	15g (½oz)	1 tablespoon
cheese, Cheddar, grated	30g (1oz)	3 level tablespoons
cocoa	30g (1oz)	3 level tablespoons
cornflour	30g (1oz)	3 level tablespoons
dried fruit	30g (1oz)	2 level tablespoons
flour, unsifted	30g (1oz)	3 level tablespoons
rice, uncooked	30g (1oz)	2 level tablespoons
rolled oats	30g (1oz)	4 level tablespoons
sugar, caster, granulated, demerara	30g (1oz)	2 level tablespoons
syrup, honey, treacle	30g (1oz)	1 level tablespoons
liquids	15ml (1½oz)	1 tablespoon
	6oml (2floz)	3 tablespoons
	150ml (¼pt)	8 tablespoons

Yeast: 1 sachet usually contains 15g (½oz) which sufficient for a 1.5 kg (3.3lb) loaf.

Juice of 1 lemon – 2-3 tablespoons. Juice of 1 lime – 1-2 tablespoons.

Unless specified, all eggs are medium or size 3.

OVEN TEMPERATURES

110°C=	225 °F, gas mark ¼, very cool
120°C =	250°F, gas mark ½
140°C =	275°F, gas mark 1, cool
150°C =	300°F, gas mark 2
160°C =	325°F, gas mark 3, moderate
180°C =	350°F, gas mark 4
190°C =	375°F, gas mark 5, moderately hot
200°C =	400°F, gas mark 6
220°C =	425°F, gas mark 7, hot
230°C =	450°F, gas mark 8
240°C =	475°F, gas mark 9, very hot
250°C =	500°F, gas mark 9